Walking on Water

Walking on Water

*"And when Peter was come down out of the |boat|,
he walked on the water, to go to Jesus."*
—Matthew 14:29

Greg Hinnant

CREATION
HOUSE
PRESS

WALKING ON WATER by Greg Hinnant
Published by Creation House Press
A part of Strang Communications Company
600 Rinehart Road
Lake Mary, Florida 32746
www.creationhouse.com

Library of Congress Catalog Card Number: 2001097463
International Standard Book Number: 0-88419-875-8

02 03 04 05 87654321
Printed in the United States of America

To
Christians everywhere
who yearn to walk stably on the
troubled waters of
life.

Acknowledgments

Most gratefully, I acknowledge the following individuals, whose faithful exercise of their gifts of "helps" (1 Cor. 12:28) enables this ministry to faithfully help the people of God. They are:

Alice W. Bosworth

Jean Brock

John J. McHugh, Jr.

Virginia G. McHugh

Kathleen E. McHugh

Phyllis H. McNeill

Mary Ann Mowery

Evelyn A. Ward

I also wish to acknowledge the fine efforts of the staff of Creation House Press, whose assistance, advice and patient attentiveness to detail have helped make this book a blessing to many. They are:

Rev. Dr. Allen Quain, Manager

Deborah Poulalian, Editor

Deborah Moss, Copyeditor

Rachel Campbell, Graphic Design

Sallie Traynor, Typesetting

Contents

PREFACE

The revelation that Jesus walked on water is nothing new. Every informed Christian knows that He did this and many other wonders. Yet the fourteenth chapter of Matthew's Gospel reveals something else that we may have overlooked: Peter also walked on water.

Matthew wrote, "And when Peter was come down out of the |boat|, *he walked on the water*" (Matt. 14:29, emphasis added). This amazing spectacle becomes even more amazing when we consider that the waters upon which Peter walked were not placid. At that moment, the Sea of Galilee was churning, rolling and foaming with a great storm. The wind was "contrary," the disciples' boat was "tossed," and the wind-whipped waves were "boisterous" (Matt. 14:24, 30). Hence, the full revelation is that Peter walked on *stormy waters* to go to Jesus. Symbolically, the Spirit of God is sending us a significant message.

When used figuratively in the Bible, waters symbolize trouble, and stormy waters (also "deep waters") symbolize great trouble. (See Psalm 69:2, 14–15.) As an apostle, Peter represents both a believer and a servant of God. His actions, therefore, speak of the overcoming Christian who continues to walk closely with Jesus in faith, peace, contentment and service when severe trials of faith, patience and loyalty come storming into his life. The spiritual implications of Peter's exploit are both challenging and comforting.

They comfort us because if Peter walked on water, so can we. By grace, through faith, as we keep our hearts focused on the Word, we can overcome life's worst buffetings. Peter's victory, albeit brief, forever proves to all downtrodden Christians that spiritual victory is indeed possible. If we will, we can have it. We too may walk with God in our most turbulent times without sinking into doubt, despair and panic. Thus the faith to imitate the essence of Peter's actions is born within us.

Peter's victory also challenges us because if we are not presently overcoming our stormy trials, the question naturally arises, Why aren't we? What is holding us back from spiritual victory? The answer may be simply a lack of knowledge: "My people are destroyed for lack of knowledge" (Hos. 4:6)—not the general knowledge of God, but the specific knowledge of how to think of and respond to the boisterous troubles we face as developing overcomers of Christ.

This book offers a number of biblical messages down this very line. Feed on them. Consider them long and consider them well. If believed and practiced, they will enable you to walk on any stormy waters that come your way . . . until He upon whom every eye of faith is focused comes.

—Greg Hinnant

Chapter One

WHY THE TROUBLE, LORD?

Lord, wherefore hast thou so |badly treated| this people?
Why is it that thou hast sent me?

—EXODUS 5:22

Shortly after Moses returned to Egypt and began helping his brethren, he met a tidal wave of trouble. (See Exodus 5:1–23.) Pharaoh flatly refused to cooperate with Jehovah's demands. Instead of releasing the Hebrews, he increased their hardships. Offended, Moses' brethren then hastily denounced his leadership, invoking judgment on their minister of deliverance and his assistant: "The LORD look upon you, and judge; because ye have made |us offensive| in the eyes of Pharaoh" (Exod. 5:21). Perplexed by his dilemma, Moses prayed, "[Lord,] why is it that thou hast sent me?" (v. 22). In so doing, Moses expressed the inevitable prayer-question of every troubled Christian's heart.

Whenever we get into trouble or trouble gets after us, the "why" question always arises—and rightfully so. While demanding specific explanations from the Almighty only earns us His silence or His rebukes, a general understanding of the reason for our trials is something we should seek after. Why? Because only spiritual understanding holds us calm in the day of trouble: "Understanding shall keep thee" (Prov. 2:11). But sadly, not all believers recognize this need.

Some Christians assume rather nonchalantly that trouble of all kinds strikes us irrespective of spiritual or moral causes, and they never give their adversities a second thought. This attitude is not wise. As Moses, we should pray for understanding. God Himself confirmed this by answering the cry of His sorely pressed deliverer. His response, "Now shalt thou see what I will do to Pharaoh" (Exod. 6:1), gave Moses the understanding he needed to stand firm against his enemy. It confirmed the key pillars of his faith, i.e., the Lord had not changed His plan—"Mission Exodus" was still on; though God permitted an unexpected flood of distress, Moses still had His full favor; Pharaoh would at last capitulate and Moses triumph; and God's powerful intervention (the plagues) to save Moses and his mission would begin soon. (See Exodus 6:1–8.) Upheld by God's reassurance, Moses walked on the troubled waters he faced. Like Moses, we must have an understanding of the troubles that buffet us.

There are at least four different kinds of troubles that visit believers. Let's examine them.

THE GENERAL TROUBLES OF LIFE

Trouble is an inescapable part of the human experience. There are only two kinds of people who are truly trouble-free: the unborn and the dead. Every other child of Adam will taste trouble periodically: "Yet man is born unto trouble, as the sparks fly upward" (Job 5:7). So the Book of Job points to the general troubles of life.

These general troubles befall large masses of people (continents, nations, provinces, cities) irrespective of their religious beliefs or lack thereof. They are sweeping adversities, such as war, economic recession and foul weather. When a blizzard hits, everyone in the storm area, whether Christian, Muslim, Buddhist or atheist, is caught in its frigid grip. When a hurricane strikes, the saved and the unsaved seek shelter together. When war is declared, the sons of both the godly and the ungodly are drafted, trained and sent.

Though troubles sometimes visit because of prolonged national sins, these general adversities have no bearing whatsoever on the faith and obedience of individuals. They are not caused by any one person's wickedness or averted by another's righteousness. Everyone is swept up in them and, to some degree, troubled until they end. Hence, they are truly inescapable.

Well, maybe not. In the latter decades of the twentieth century, the National Aeronautics and Space Administration (NASA) devised a way to deliver humans from earthly troubles. They sent them to the moon. Yet, despite their thrilling deliverance, the astronauts who took advantage of that means of escape soon returned to the rest of us—and to the general troubles of life.

THE TROUBLES OF DISOBEDIENT CHRISTIANS

As heavenly Father of every born-again person, God has certain obligations toward us. He provides for us the necessities of life. By His Word He strengthens and encourages us. By His Spirit He teaches us and comforts us. By the visitation of His Son He has given us the ultimate example. By His angels He protects us. By His presence He loves us and fellowships freely with us. So are His fatherly ways with all His children who seek and obey Him. To His disobedient ones, however,

He reveals a different aspect of His divine fatherhood, namely, His chastening: "Despise not thou the chastening of the Lord" (Heb. 12:5; see vv. 6–17).

If we disobey God's Word or the leading of His Spirit, He immediately sends us a word of correction or rebuke: "And thine ears shall hear a word behind thee, saying, This is the way, walk ye in it, when ye turn [out of the straight way of obedience] to the right hand, and when ye turn to the left" (Isa. 30:21). If we continue to disobey, He gets after us with His rod of correction. Stressful, disruptive troubles come to vex us, as they did the Israelites in the days of their rebellion: "And in those times there was no peace…but great vexations were upon all…for God did vex them with all adversity" (2 Chron. 15:5–6). If our rebellion persists, our heavenly Father sends very serious troubles upon us.

Unlike the typical parent of this Laodicean age, He loves us enough to do *whatever* is necessary to bring us to our senses. Love distresses us now so sin won't destroy us later. So the apostle wrote, "But when we are judged, we are chastened of the Lord, that we should not be condemned with the world" (1 Cor. 11:32). The heavenly Father has used trouble to jolt many of our spiritual ancestors.

Jonah's rebellion forced God to put him in a very uncomfortable place—a fish's stomach. He wouldn't have experienced his unique "underwater adventure" if he had obeyed God's call to preach to Nineveh. Jacob's slowness to return to Bethel led to his daughter's rape at Shechem; Dinah's humiliation and the subsequent crimes of Jacob's sons would never have happened if Jacob had been at Bethel where he belonged. There would have been no strife between Hagar and Sarah or mockery of Isaac by Ishmael if Abraham had not become unequally yoked to Sarah's handmaid; he reaped bitter fruits from the marital disobedience he sowed.

Friend, have you been visited by the heavenly Father's

4

rod? If you are caught in a great dilemma because you have disobeyed His will, heed this humbling-yet-simple advice: *Reverse your course.* Resolve by obedience the perplexities you have created by disobedience. Go to Nineveh, the place where God called you to serve. Return to Bethel, the close daily fellowship with Jesus to which the Spirit has been calling you. Put away Hagar, that unsanctioned relationship in which you have entangled yourself. Then deliverance will overtake you as suddenly as it did Jonah. Your mighty Redeemer will kindly thrust you from the depths of your troubled waters to the shores of another opportunity. And the word of the Lord will come to you a "second time" (Jon. 3:1). (See chapter 6, pages 58–59.)

THE TROUBLES OF OBEDIENT CHRISTIANS (DEVELOPING DISCIPLES)

When as Christians we commit ourselves to a lifestyle of seriously seeking God's Word and obeying it, we enter into discipleship. Said Christ, "If ye continue in my word, then are ye my disciples indeed" (John 8:31). As we begin our personal march toward the promised land of spiritual maturity, trouble meets us. The twin sons of Anak, Tribulation and Persecution, attack and withstand us to keep us from tasting the rewards of "doers of the word" (James 1:22).

This resistance is not by chance. It is sent directly from the diabolical troubler himself, Satan. Christ taught plainly that whenever we receive His Word in our hearts, "Satan cometh immediately" to try to steal the Word sown (Mark 4:15). Satan knows well that if we continue to feed upon the Scriptures daily and obey them at every opportunity, we will develop steadily as disciples of the Lord. Eventually we will become established in a stable, daily walk with God, who will then declare us approved of God and fit for the Master's use. The Deliverer will then begin using us to release many spiritual captives—souls formerly bound and oppressed by Satan. The enemy loathes such an eventuality. To prevent it, therefore, he attacks developing disciples. His aim is very simple: to keep us from becoming rooted in God's Word, established in God's ways and fruitful in His service.

To achieve this, Satan uses the strategy of offense. Describing the danger of our spiritual development being cut short by satanic offenses, Jesus said, "When tribulation or persecution ariseth because of the word, |immediately| he [the developing disciple] is offended" (Matt. 13:21). By "offended" Jesus means *spiritually stumbled*. Satan's methods of stumbling us are very predictable. He moves unbelievers or carnal Christians to treat us unfairly or to criticize, insult or slander us. He then tries to fill our minds with thoughts of anger, hoping we will harbor unforgiveness or, better yet, revenge toward our offenders in defiance of Jesus' teaching on forgiveness. (See Mark 11:25–26.) And he always implants the idea, however subtle, that God has let us down—"How could God let this happen to me?"—hoping that, with our self-pity stirred, we will harbor resentment toward God for allowing us to be mistreated. (See Job 1:11; 2:5.) Such unspiritual thinking is proof that we suffer from biblical amnesia: We have completely forgotten Jesus' numerous New Testament warnings that earnest Christians will be hated, maligned and betrayed for His name's sake; that tribulation and persecution will come for His Word's sake; that if the world called Him Beelzebub and stripped Him of His rights, how much more will it disrespect and likewise mistreat us, His students, etc. If we allow anger at God and man to rest in us, we sin against Jesus and His Words, and roots of bitterness begin growing in our hearts. A slow, sad process of spiritual self-destruction then follows.

Christian self-opposition usually unfolds in this manner. Once offended, we gradually lose interest in the things of

God and cease drawing near to the Lord daily in Bible meditation and prayer. Simultaneously we stop desiring fellowship with strong believers and lose interest in church activities that are spiritual in nature. With this, all real spiritual development ceases. Once our spiritual growth ceases, we do not remain as we are; immediately, spiritual degeneration begins. And if this isn't corrected, full-blown backsliding soon sets in. In that condition, obviously, we will never again be useful to Christ, barring repentance. And the Christian service contest is over. Satan wins; we lose.

This strategy of offense explains why Potiphar's wife falsely accused Joseph. Satan moved her to do so, hoping to embitter and destroy God's chosen vessel while he was still developing. God then would never have been able to raise him to power and through him "save |many| people alive" (Gen. 50:20).

THE TROUBLES OF FRUITFUL CHRISTIAN WORKERS

By "fruitful Christian worker" we mean anyone called, prepared and sent by God to minister His Word in the power of the Spirit. These may sow the imperishable seed in any of a number of ways.

Fruitful Christian workers may be pastors, teachers, evangelists, prophets or apostles, or others who closely support or assist these in their ministries. Sadly, far too many in Christian ministry today are laboring without a genuine call from God. They have called themselves or others have called them, but the Lord's seal is not upon their foreheads, nor is His Spirit's witness upon their words and works. The enemy does not bother these Ahimaazes for, quite frankly, he likes them as they are. (See 2 Samuel 18:19–32.) In their self-led state they create more havoc than harvest in God's field. Possessing little light, they dispel little darkness. Against such workers as these, the rulers of darkness wage no war. But God-called, God-prepared, Spirit-gifted, Spirit-led Christian workers are quite a different story.

The enemy hates effective sowers of truth with a special passion and reserves for them his cruelest attacks. Why? Simply because they disrupt his kingdom daily, ever shining the light that spoils his darkness. Unlike false ministers who take honor unto themselves, these are called of God as was Aaron. Their labors are "not in vain" for they are careful to minister always "in the Lord" (1 Cor. 15:58). They work not merely for the Lord of the Harvest but in Him and with Him, "the Lord working with them" (Mark 16:20). When they speak, He speaks through them. When they act in His name, He in whom they abide acts through them. Consequently, eternal results are registered in heaven daily by their labors. Because these ministers are extraordinarily used of God, Satan exerts extraordinary pressure on them. In short, he saves his worst troubles for God's best servants. We need look no further than Scripture for abundant proof of this.

Through John the Baptist God moved the chosen nation to repentance; the enemy then moved Herod to arrest, jail and at last behead the uncompromising prophet. Through the apostles God turned the first-century world upside down. The accuser of the brethren retaliated by turning their personal lives upside down: James was slain with the sword; Peter was imprisoned and held for execution; John was exiled on the Isle of Patmos; and Paul, whose amazing revelations and spiritual powers delivered multitudes, had a demon assigned to him to stir up trouble day and night. Speaking for his peers, Paul wrote, "For I think that God hath set forth us, the apostles, last...we are...buffeted, and have no certain dwelling place...being reviled, we bless; being persecuted, we |endure| it; being defamed, we entreat" (1 Cor. 4:9–13).

Why did the enemy ill-treat these fruitful Christian workers? To end their fruitful service. He hoped to do this by forcing them to make one of two ministerially fatal errors:

1. Compromise their message
2. Altogether quit their work

Had they so yielded, they would have quenched the river of the Spirit flowing through them. And despite their past fruitfulness, God could not have continued to work powerfully through them to deliver needy souls and establish them in Christ.

~

When troubles (trials) call, it is vital that you understand the basic reason for their visit. The difference between spiritual success and failure depends on it.

One little bit of timely understanding may inspire you to overcome the waves that buffet you. For instance, to discover that your devotion or service is seriously bothering the enemy is an inspiring revelation that may spur you on to even more fruitful service. It certainly did for Nehemiah.

At some point in his conflict with the Samaritans, Nehemiah realized that all the Samaritans' threats were aimed at one target—weakening him and his workers so they would stop rebuilding the wall of Jerusalem: "For they all made us afraid, saying, Their hands shall be weakened from the work, that it is not done" (Neh. 6:9). Alertly he recognized what this meant: Satan, the Samaritans' invisible inspirer, was highly displeased with his works; hence, those works must have been highly pleasing to God, whose will Satan perpetually opposes. Inspired by this lone, tiny thought, Nehemiah immediately prayed for more strength and resolved to work even harder: "Now therefore, O God, strengthen my hands." What followed is remarkable. Despite tremendous opposition, the Jews' productivity increased, and the wall of Jerusalem was finished with amazing speed in only fifty-two days.

On the other hand, misunderstanding your troubles may cause you to stumble, and thus lose the race that is set before you. If God is chastening you, for example, and you mistake His correction for satanic persecution, you delay the thing you need most—your conviction of sin that leads you to confession and repentance. As long as you abide in self-justification and self-deception you prolong your distress, for the holy heavenly Father cannot release you from His chastisement until you humbly tell Him the truth. For that you must come to the point of "if": "*If* we confess our sins, he is faithful and just to forgive us our sins, and to cleanse us from all unrighteousness" (1 John 1:9, emphasis added). The longer you take to do this, the longer you delay your spiritual recovery.

There are other ways misunderstanding may ensnare you. If Satan is harassing you because you are diligently seeking and obeying God's Word, watch that you don't mistake his resistance for God's correction. If so deceived, you will draw back from the full discipleship you were fast pursuing. And as stated earlier, unless you become established in His Word, God cannot approve you for His service. Trees of righteousness must be well rooted to bear fruit and withstand storms. Later in your Christian experience, if demons buffet you mercilessly because God is using your ministry powerfully, you must not through excessive introspection mistake your "thorns" for arrows of divine judgment. If so, you will become discouraged and stop fighting the good fight. Then many needy souls will fail for want of your help, and you will forfeit your crown of glory. And why? Because you misunderstood the cause of your trouble.

Still other perplexing situations may buffet and threaten to overflow you. In his epistle, Peter warned us of "manifold trials": "Though now for a season...ye are in heaviness through *manifold |trials|*" (1 Pet. 1:6, emphasis added). Several translations (New American Standard and Modern

Language Bible, for example) render the word *manifold* (Greek, *poikilos*) as *various. The New Testament in Modern English* by J. B. Phillips renders "manifold trials" as "all kinds of trials." Clearly, then, the Spirit reveals that at times we are confronted by multiplied or multifaceted trials—several trials running concurrently yet for different reasons. In these complex situations, the causes of trouble may be mixed.

For instance, while in a long trial that has come because you are generally obedient to Christ, you may refuse to keep the Word in an isolated area of your thought or conduct. Hence, the Lord may chasten you for your disobedience in that matter, while the cause of your larger trial remains unchanged. For ten years David was persecuted by King Saul for righteousness' sake and forced to live in the wilderness. If during this time he had disobeyed Abigail's warning and taken vengeance on Nabal (1 Sam. 25), the Lord would have chastened David for his disobedience concerning Nabal, even though his larger troubles with Saul remained due to his righteousness and the divine call on his life.

Conversely, while being chastened for your past persistent disobedience to God, you may suffer rejection solely for Christ's sake. When Israel rebelled against God at Kadesh-barnea by refusing to go to war to possess the land of Canaan, God sentenced the nation to wander aimlessly in the wilderness for thirty-eight and a half more years. During this lengthy trial, which was caused by their disobedience, a shorter conflict arose. Balak, king of Moab, hired the prophet Balaam in an attempt to curse the Israelites, who by then were camped nearby. (See Numbers 22.) Although the Israelites' wanderings were caused by their sin, surprisingly, Balak's move to destroy them was not. It arose solely because they were God's chosen people and would yet do God's will. Note that in Balaam's majestic prophetic utterances God speaks of the Israelites' righteousness (legal justification before God) and ultimate lofty destiny, not their present sinfulness (Num. 23–24). So, we see the differing causes of Israel's "manifold trials." While sin caused their long-term tribulation in the wilderness, righteousness caused their short-term trouble with Balak. Take these lessons to heart.

The next time trouble strikes, do not make a foolishly quick assumption as to its cause. Follow Moses' example instead. Ask the Lord why it has come upon you, and don't stop seeking Him until you have a clear, confirmed answer from on high. You will find you can overcome any trouble—whether by repentance or perseverance—if only you are willing to see God and His purpose in the thing that has touched your life.

Chapter Two

SEEING GOD
IN EVERYTHING

In all thy ways acknowledge him.

—PROVERBS 3:6

To overcome the troubles that buffet us as Christian disciples, we must learn to see God in everything that touches our lives, or, in the inspired words of King Solomon, "In all thy ways acknowledge him [God]" (Prov. 3:6). Simply put, we must believe and acknowledge that God permits every situation we meet. If we refuse this first step, we cannot run, and so will never win, the race set before us. Instead of finishing our courses as overcomers, we will be overcome and spiritually finished by our trials. Instead of walking on water, we will sink fast into the depths of spiritual uselessness. To avoid this, let's examine ourselves honestly.

The truth is we have no difficulty seeing God in good

things. When success or prosperity comes our way, we immediately acknowledge God and identify our blessings as answers to prayer or rewards from on high. But too often our view of adverse situations is different. When troubles visit, we immediately become faith-blind; strangely, we seem no longer able to see Him who is invisible. And the first person we acknowledge in our trials is usually diabolical, not divine: "An enemy hath done this" (Matt. 13:28). Although *Diabolos* is surely present and working, we must learn to look beyond him and focus on this vital truth:

OUR DIFFICULTIES ARE PERMITTED
BY THE SAME GOD WHO SENDS
OUR BLESSINGS. THEY TOO
COME FROM ON HIGH.

Troubles, then, require us to take a new viewpoint if we are to keep the faith. By a conscious choice, we must learn to receive our troubles from God just as surely as we do our blessings. Job did so.

When experiencing the worst kind of troubles, Job said, "What? Shall we receive good at the hand of God, and shall we not receive evil?" (Job 2:10). In other words, "Should we not acknowledge that God has as much control over bad things as He does over good things?" To have the faith and patience of Job, we must acquire his attitude, one that sees God's hand in the unpleasant as readily as it does in the pleasant. We may not understand everything (or sometimes anything) He is doing, but we must accept that He has allowed the situation at hand. To this end God has given us four special Bible passages.

More than any others, these scriptures help us see the

Lord in everything we experience daily. They are each based upon the conviction that absolutely nothing—from the best to the worst events—can touch us unless our faithful and loving heavenly Father personally permits it. They each employ the use of all-inclusive language, such as "everything," "all," "all thy ways" and "all things"; hence, they take into account truly *everything* we experience and leave nothing excluded from their scope. And they are absolutely fireproof—tested by fire; they may be trusted to see you through even your fieriest ordeals. Here are their expositions.

1 Thessalonians 5:18

In everything give thanks; for this is the will of God in Christ Jesus concerning you.

This verse is so simple it needs little explanation. Our problems arise not in understanding but in accepting all that it implies.

The first part of this verse is a command. "In" the midst of every circumstance, whether a blessing or a test, we are to "give thanks" to God. Before we know why God has permitted a given situation, before we understand what He is doing in us, for us or through us, before we see how He will bear fruit or bring glory to Himself, we are to simply *give thanks*: "Thank You, Jesus." This is the "sacrifice of praise" that the writer to the Hebrews exhorts us to give "continually." (See Hebrews 13:15.) This blind thanksgiving is an expression of faith in God and submission to His will that exercises, and so increases, our attitude of acceptance. Note also the Spirit's use of the all-inclusive word *everything*: "In everything." When God says "everything," He includes all possible circumstances: "in all circumstances," (as the New International Version translates it). So no situation can arise that this verse does not cover. Here God tells us what to do.

15

Next He tells us why we should do this. His revelation is simple but revolutionary: "for this is the will of God in Christ Jesus concerning you." This revelation has a twofold meaning.

First, it means that it is God's will that we be thankful. And, conversely, it is *not* His will that we murmur and complain. This is the lesson taught time and again in the record of the Israelites' wilderness wanderings. So grieved was God by their constant complaints (all of which slandered Him for His care of them) that He finally executed judgment upon them. Hence, the New Testament exhorts us, "Neither murmur ye, as some of them also murmured, and were destroyed by the destroyer" (1 Cor. 10:10).

Complaining in every circumstance has become so ubiquitous that it seems to be the modern American pastime. Just name your topic—weather, wages, politics and so forth—and the average American will name his complaint. Because God seeks to root this nonconstructive criticism out of Christians, He commands us to give thanks in all things. Every time we obey, complaining dies within us. By a law of spiritual displacement, the spirit of thanksgiving drives the spirit of murmuring from our personalities. Thus we do, and are, the will of God.

Second, this verse reveals that every circumstance we meet daily is God's will for us. Note the link between the words *everything* and *this*: "In *everything* give thanks, for *this* is the will of God in Christ Jesus concerning you" (emphasis added). As seen in Job's experience, God overrules our lives in complete omnipotence. (See Job 1:10, 12.) Nothing can touch us (our possessions, relationships, homes, bodies) unless He approves its passage through the hedge of angelic protection that surrounds us. So everything that reaches the shores of our personal experience—even tribulation and persecution sent directly from Satan—is God's will for us *by the time it meets us*. It's either His perfect will or His permissive will. Let's

16

examine the difference between the perfect and the permissive will of God.

God's perfect will occurs when our circumstances are "Edenic"—similar to His original plan for mankind. There is no willful sin, sorrow or grief, nor is there any trouble, rejection or want. Our lives are filled with order, peace, prosperity, growth, health, love and joy. In these ideal conditions the Lord is glorified and pleased, for He "hath pleasure in the prosperity of his servant" (Ps. 35:27). And we are perfectly happy. We wouldn't even think of resisting or complaining.

God's permissive will, however, is quite different. It occurs whenever God *permits*, or allows, adversity to come upon us. The Edenic fades and the chaotic erupts as things outside God's perfect will break through our protective hedge and invade our lives. God does not intend for these troubles to remain, but He permits them temporarily to test our faith and loyalty to Him. Every such intrusion of trouble is a subtle divine message. God is silently challenging us to overcome— to first of all see and accept His hand in our circumstances and *give thanks*; then to seek and obey His guidance and rise above the chaos He has permitted.

For example, God permitted the Amalekites to destroy David's home at Ziklag and capture his wives and children. (See 1 Samuel 30:1–6.) Though from one perspective this was God's disciplinary judgment against David, who had fallen into unbelief sixteen months earlier and left Israel without divine authorization (1 Sam. 27:1–7), it was also a great test of David's faith and courage. Would he turn back to the Lord in his day of trouble, or would he turn away, permanently offended with Love? Apparently, David saw the hand of God in both his discipline and his test, for he promptly prayed, seeking restoration and guidance (1 Sam. 30:6), then pursued the Amalekites and recovered all (vv. 7–19). So his life was reestablished in God's perfect will.

Job's trials are another example of the permissive will of God. God permitted very baffling contradictions to befall Job solely to test his faith and endurance. In two shocking blitzkrieg attacks, Satan took everything from Job—first his possessions and children, and later his health and friends. Job's initial reaction to his cruel chaos was significant and instructive. Believing that God controlled everything that touched his life, Job first accepted his calamity as from God, insisting that the Lord of his prosperity was still present in his adversity: "The LORD gave, and the LORD hath taken away; blessed be the name of the LORD" (Job 1:21). Thus he saw God in everything, acknowledging that even diabolical attacks, once they receive divine permission to visit, are from the Lord. The sacred writer captured this thought when twice he penned the revelation, "So Satan went forth *from the presence of the LORD*" (Job 1:12, emphasis added; see Job 2:7). Without this foundational belief, Job's house of faith would have quickly collapsed. He would never have lived to see his captivity turned and his life reestablished in the perfect will of God (Job 42:10–17). It is the same with us.

If we are to successfully endure our seasons in the permissive will of God, we must see "everything" as being, in some way, the will of God for us in Christ Jesus. If it is a blessing, it is God's will, freely given us to enjoy. If it is a baffling contradiction to faith, it is God's will, sent to try, and so increase, our faith. If it is a delay or interruption, it is God's will, designed to stretch, and so enlarge, our patience. If our self-appointed plans fail, it is God's will, so that we may learn to trust only in His plans. If it is an offense, it is God's will, so that we may learn to forgive. If it is a rejection or betrayal, it is God's will, so that we may have a cross of our own to bear...and one day a great reward. Tremendous spiritual growth follows when we embrace this revelation.

James 1:2–4

**My brethren, count it all joy when ye fall into
| various trials |, knowing this, that the | testing |
of your faith worketh patience. But let patience
have her perfect work, that ye may be perfect
and entire, | lacking | nothing.**

Through James, the Spirit forewarns us that we will "fall into," or suddenly experience, various trials in our Christian walk on a daily basis. "When" we do so, or the instant our trials arise, we should "count it all joy"; that is, we should quickly and gladly accept our unpleasant interruptions (not some, but "all" of them). Again, this takes every situation into account. To meet all our sudden trials with joyful acceptance is extremely difficult. What will inspire us to do this? Only the faith that sees God in every situation we meet. Accordingly, the Spirit gives us a revelation to build this faith on: "Knowing [realizing and believing] this, that the | testing | of your faith worketh patience" (James 1:3). This implies that our trying circumstances are not accidental but providential. Our heavenly Father permits them—even designs them—as tests of our faith. They enable us to prove that we trust Him, and they are the only means by which we may increase our trust in Him, as well as our patience.

Then the Teacher gives a second command: "But let patience have her perfect work" (v. 4). That is, be perfectly patient in your trial. "Let," or allow, the patience of Jesus in you to fully have its way. If we believe that our unplanned distresses are part of God's plans for us, it is easy to "let patience have her perfect work." In complete surrender to God we simply maintain fellowship with Jesus and learn to endure. According to the late Mrs. C. Nuzum, a Christian writer and missionary to Mexico, *to endure* means "to move steadily on in the way, work and will of the Lord, even when things are very different from what we wish them to be."[1] As we so wait, our patience, or ability to endure, grows until, at last, it is finished: "Let your endurance be a finished product" (James 1:4, MOFFATT).

To further motivate us to "let," a second revelation is given: "that ye [your character] may be perfect and entire, |lacking| nothing" (v. 4). This reveals that our heavenly Father uses our various trials to develop our Christian character to its fullest extent.

All this—the proving of our faith, the perfecting of our patience, the maturing of our character—begins with, and so depends upon, seeing our Father's hand in "all" the trials we fall into, large and small. No matter how accidentally they may seem to arise, this passage asserts that He and His purposes are behind them.

Proverbs 3:5–6

**Trust in the LORD with all thine heart, and
lean not unto thine own understanding.
In all thy ways acknowledge him, and
he shall direct thy paths.**

We have here instructions for divine guidance. To be led of God we must do certain things.

First, we must choose to trust—lean on, rely on, place confidence in—the Lord: "Trust in the LORD." And this trust must be total. We must be prepared, when necessary, to go beyond the limits of our own conservative wisdom: "with all thine heart." Second, we must not allow carnal reasoning (our ideas or others' suggestions) to interfere with our obedience to the Lord's clearly revealed will: "and lean not unto thine own understanding." We must always remember that God's intelligence is infinitely higher than ours. Third, we must acknowledge God's presence and control in all our circumstances: "In all thy ways acknowledge him." Again, note the use of the blanket term "all"; therefore, every circumstance is covered by this verse. If we do all these things, God will guide us perfectly: "And he shall direct thy paths."

The third instruction above, which is the focus of this chapter, is perhaps the most important one. The *only* way to trust the Lord with "all thine heart" and therefore avoid dependence upon human reasoning is to acknowledge God's invisible hand in "all thy ways." To do that we must constantly remember God's omnipresence and omnipotence, that He is ever-present and all-powerful, always. Everything beyond our control is still within His control. Even the smallest details are ordered by His all-seeing eye and guided by His unseen touch. We must train ourselves, therefore, to acknowledge God in all the conditions that surround us, such as weather, the timing of events, people's actions and reactions and seemingly accidental meetings.

For instance, when people are drawn to us, we should acknowledge God; He is giving us favor. When they reject us without cause, we should acknowledge God; He is withholding favor. For some reason He does not want us united with them at present. When someone comes to us with bad news, we should acknowledge God; He wants us to be aware of the problem for prayer and/or action. When we see our secret petitions fulfilled, we should acknowledge God; our Father, who sees in secret, has rewarded us openly. If practiced, this spiritual exercise will significantly increase our ability to discern God in everyday events.

Romans 8:28
And we know that all things work together for good to them that love God, to them who are the called according to his purpose.

Note two things here. First, the "good" described here does not result from the working of some unknown universal benevolent force. It results from the personal working of our Father-God. He is the great Worker of all things. The *New Scofield Study Bible* says early manuscripts support the understanding that God is the force who causes *all* things to work for *our* good: Scofield noted, "Some early manuscripts read, 'God worketh all things together for good.'" The New American Standard text also brings out this fact: "God causes all things to work together for good."

Second, we see yet another all-inclusive phrase, "all things." Here, however, this phrase must be qualified. Widely misunderstood, this verse is often said to teach that all things are working for the good of all people everywhere. Some even claim our sins work for our good. But this simply is not so. Our personal disobedience to God, which involves matters within our control, always works for our grief and loss, never our good. Even when we glean valuable lessons from our failures, obedience is always the better and less costly way for us to learn. So, this verse really speaks of "all things" *beyond our control.*

Also, some apparently fail to understand, or they choose to ignore, the two key conditional phrases attached to this promise: "to them that love God, to them who are the called according to his purpose." *This means if we are obedient to God's Word and pursuing His call on our lives—and these are rather large "ifs"—He causes every event in our lives to work together toward the good end He has predestined for us.* How do we derive this interpretation?

Well, Jesus repeatedly equated love for Him with obedience to His Word. (See John 14:15, 21, 23.) We know, therefore, that those who obey the scriptural light they have are the ones who truly love God. This immediately disqualifies the disobedient Christian from the promise of Romans 8:28, for a person who habitually disobeys God's Word is not a lover of God. The second phrase, "called according to his purpose," implies more than being called by God; it suggests conscious cooperation with that call. That is, we live for God's purpose, not our own selfish ends. So Christians who refuse to follow the leading of the Spirit are also disqualified. Those who go their own way and do their own thing, even if they are otherwise obedient to the Word, are not "called according to his purpose [His specific will or plan for them]." And God is not causing all things to work together for their good. Still more clarification is needed.

This text does not teach that all things that touch our lives are good. Obviously, many of them are not. It teaches that God is working them "together" with other events— often involving people and places unknown to us at present— to bring us to a good end. By "good" God means two things.

First, He is working toward humanly good ends. God leads obedient ones to the eventual fulfillment of their hearts' desires. (See Psalm 37:4.) His workings bring about the very blessings we need and desire most as men and women sojourning in this present world. He caused the distresses of bereavement, immigration, poverty and hard work to work together for Ruth's good when, at last, she met and married Boaz, gave birth to Obed and thus entered the most honorable family line in Israel.

Second, God works always toward divinely good ends. In fact, the verse following Romans 8:28 plainly states the good purpose God has for every Christian. It is that we be "conformed to the image of his Son" (Rom. 8:29). Only Christians whose characters have been made like Christ's will rule and reign with Him eternally. To become like the Man of Sorrows, we must in some measure go the way He went. We must bear our crosses as He bore His, willingly enduring whatever rejections, humiliations or defeats God sends us. As

23

we do so, the Holy Spirit conforms our characters to that of Christ. So God causes "all things," even our sorrows, to serve this, His supreme purpose in our lives.

~

Sustained meditation inclines us toward, and so creates, the reality of what we meditate upon. God ordered Joshua to meditate constantly in His law that he might obey His law: "This book of the law...thou shalt meditate therein day and night, that thou mayest observe to do according to all that is written therein" (Josh. 1:8). Humbly, Joshua complied, meditating in God's law day and night. The result was an extraordinarily obedient life: "As the Lord commanded Moses...so did Joshua; he left nothing undone of all that the Lord commanded Moses" (Josh. 11:15). Should we not, with childlike simplicity, follow Joshua's example?

The purpose of this chapter is to present the four texts mentioned above, that you may henceforth meditate in these inspired phrases:

- "In *everything*...this is the will of God."
- "Count it *all* joy."
- "In *all* thy ways acknowledge him."
- "God worketh *all* things together for good."

As you ponder and speak them time and again, the truths they convey will possess you and incline you to obey. Inspired by a new viewpoint, your heart will begin discerning God, however slowly, in every situation you encounter. This will make it much easier for you to pray, and so understand, the cause of your troubles, as suggested in chapter 1. The result will be, well, overcoming.

When stormy waters buffet, you will calmly stand still, saying, "It is the Lord; let him do what seemeth to him good" (1 Sam. 3:18); then you will rise and conquer. When events take strange turns and waves of discouragement overflow you,

you will hear a still, small voice saying, "This thing is from me" (1 Kings 12:24), and, encouraged, you will pray for further orders, obey them and walk atop your surging troubles. To then maintain your victory, you must learn to never be discouraged as God undertakes to entirely sanctify you.

Chapter Three

DON'T GET DOWN
ON YOURSELF

It is enough! Now, O LORD, take away my life; for I am
not better than my fathers.

—1 KINGS 19:4

Sanctification is the process by which God takes
Christians in hand and makes them holy. Accordingly,
Paul prayed, "And the very God of peace sanctify you wholly
…your whole spirit and soul and body…preserved blameless
unto the coming of our Lord Jesus Christ" (1 Thess. 5:23,
emphasis added). This process of inward and outward purifi-
cation moves just as fast as we let it. If we are willing and obedient, our spiritual growth is steady. If we are rebellious, years
may pass without any real progress occurring. If we live
between these two extremes, we grow, but slowly.

In the ups and downs of typical Christian experience, we
often fail: "For in many things we |all stumble|" (James 3:2).

God's standards are high, and we frequently come short, tripped up by "the sin which doth so easily beset us" (Hebrews 12:1). At times, even the most earnest disciples manage to hinder their own sanctification.

How do we do this? By doubting, like Peter, we sink into unbelief and falter. (See Matthew 14:22–33.) By fretting, like John, we become so irritated that we call down fiery judgment on those who don't readily receive our Lord. (See Luke 9:51–56.) By complaining, like the Israelites, we speak evil of the good things God has provided for us. (See Numbers 11:4–9.) By impatience, like King Saul, we break out and do what God's Word clearly forbids. (See 1 Samuel 13:1–14.) By panic, like the apostles, we collapse in the stormy trial and foolishly accuse God of indifference: "Carest thou not that we perish?" (Mark 4:38). Due to sheer exhaustion, like David, our faith faints and we believe, and live, a lie for a season: "I shall now perish one day by the hand of Saul" (1 Sam. 27:1).

Whatever the cause of these occasional failures, the psychological reaction felt in the soul of the earnest Christian is sure. He will hate himself for it: "Oh, wretched man that I am!" (Rom. 7:24). And if he does not quickly confess his sins to God and receive forgiveness, he will fall into the dangerous pit of discouragement. Its deadly mire has hindered some of God's greatest servants.

The mighty prophet Elijah became so disgusted with himself one day that he cried, "Now, O LORD, take away my life; for I am not better than my fathers" (1 Kings 19:4). His hasty summary of his life simply could not have been accurate. If he were as bad as he claimed, if he had not attained to the godliness of his forefathers, God would never have called him to the prophetic office. That Elijah was anointed was proof that his spiritual life was approved unto God; the Spirit doesn't rest on disobedient lives, but on characters ("tabernacles") built according to the will of God. (See Exodus

40:33–35.) Obviously, Elijah's brief autobiographical sketch was tainted with the emotion of the moment. He was so angry with himself for having fled at Jezebel's death threat that all his previous spiritual progress seemed worthless. But it wasn't worthless; it was *priceless*. Very, very few, before or after Elijah, have walked as closely with God or stood as strongly for Him. Elijah's life had not been a failure; he just *felt* as if it had.

If we have never felt similarly sharp pains of self-condemnation, it may be because we have never realized just how high God's standards are. We think only in terms of the externals. We assume, for instance, that if we avoid the more obvious sins and full-blown apostasy, all will be well with us in the end. We're saved, we're "in," so what is there to worry about? The casual Christian never realizes the depth to which the Spirit of Truth wants to cleanse him. The Sanctifier seeks "truth in the inward parts" (Ps. 51:6). "Piercing even to the dividing asunder of soul and spirit," He discerns the very "thoughts and intents of the heart" (Heb. 4:12). And He will not leave us alone until every desire, every motive, yes, "every thought" is in submissive agreement with God's will: "bringing into captivity every thought to the obedience of Christ" (2 Cor. 10:5). So He leads us as we cleanse ourselves from "all filthiness of the flesh and spirit" (2 Cor. 7:1). If we don't even know that such lofty standards exist, how can we recognize our failure to meet them? Then once we see God's standards and begin seeking them, there is another issue we must face: We must learn to conquer the discouragement that arises when we occasionally fail. For that, we must possess and practice the grace of spiritual resilience.

The Book of Proverbs urges us to bounce back after every spiritual defeat: "A just man falleth seven times, and riseth up again" (Prov. 24:16). But why, or how, does the proverbial "just man" repeatedly recover from his failures? He does so because his faith in God's mercy gives him a resilient attitude. He believes God's promises of forgiveness: "He that covereth his sins shall not prosper, but whoso confesseth and forsaketh them shall have mercy" (Prov. 28:13); and again, "For thou, Lord, art good, and ready to forgive, and plenteous in mercy unto all those who call upon thee" (Ps. 86:5). So whenever he fails to meet the standard of the Word, the just man makes an efficient spiritual business transaction. He quickly repents and confesses his sins to God; then, confident that he is faithfully forgiven and cleansed, he draws nigh his Forgiver, worships and moves on in life and duty. (Consider King David's exemplary spiritual recovery after the death of his firstborn child by Bathsheba; see 2 Samuel 12:20.) He refuses to condemn anyone, including himself, whom God has forgiven and restored. This is the lesson God taught Peter: "What God hath cleansed, that call not thou common" (Acts 10:15). Paul even wrote, "Yea, I judge not mine own self" (1 Cor. 4:3). In this way, resilient souls recover quickly from their falls. Their stumbling then becomes less frequent until they are established in an even, steady walk with the Lord: "And they shall walk, and not faint" (Isa. 40:31). But not every Christian practices spiritual resilience.

A surprisingly high percentage of us prefer to put ourselves down, at least for a few hours or days. Yet if a Christian punishes himself by indulging in the memory of the seven times he has failed, he is sure to fall the eighth time. Why? Because attitude determines spiritual direction. As long as our attitude is slanted downward with self-condemnation, we cannot rise up to walk victoriously. We must correct our attitude first. Or to put it in American slang, we must quit "bellyaching." Then we may again make sustained progress in our walk with God and in our ongoing war with the enemy.

Well aware of the debilitating effects of despair, our adversary, the devil, sends a flood of condemning thoughts against the thresholds of our minds whenever we fall. We must recognize that this flow of supernegativism leads only to self-opposition. Rather than motivate positive changes, strengthen faith or inspire praise, such thoughts worsen our condition. They paralyze all our constructive actions, weaken our faith and prompt us to sullenness and murmuring. This perpetuates our misery of self-disappointment and creates new failures, as our inferior feelings inspire more inferior living. And the longer we remain down on ourselves, the further down we go.

This depression is also deadly, for there is always the possibility we will never recover ourselves. If it is not checked, self-depreciation may lead to such serious failures that our potential for further usefulness by God is destroyed: "lest perhaps such a one should be swallowed up with overmuch sorrow" (2 Cor. 2:7). In Elijah's case, his depression provoked him to pray rashly that he might die. God then responded by choosing Elisha as his replacement. (See 1 Kings 19:16, 19–21.) Consequently, though he had successfully uprooted the worship of Baal, Elijah never led the revival of true Judaism he had long awaited. Elisha assumed his office and Elijah went home to be with the Lord. (See 2 Kings 2:1–15.)

Lest we repeat Elijah's failure, we must learn to reverse the deadly downward trend of discouragement. We may do so by simply following the instructions given us in Scripture. First, we must rein in our thoughts, casting down every dread and taking captive every thought of condemnation: "Casting down imaginations, and every high thing…and bringing into captivity every thought to the obedience of Christ" (2 Cor. 10:3–5). Second, we must take God at His Word in the matter of forgiveness. He plainly promises every Christian:

> If we confess our sins, he is faithful and just to forgive us our sins, and to cleanse us from all unrighteousness.
> —1 John 1:9

31

The only question remaining is, Will we believe Him and accept His gracious offer? That is, when discouraged, will we promptly transact spiritual business with God according to this promise? If so, we will grow in the grace of spiritual resilience—and in our ability to walk on water. If not, down we will go into a powerful vortex of sorrow and senseless waste, and who knows if we will ever escape its hold? For such folly there can be only one reason: pride. The spirit that refuses to accept what it does not deserve will never receive anything from God for, in the strictest sense, none of us deserves anything but judgment.

So the next time you fail God and want to kick yourself, don't. Don't waste thirty seconds of your, and God's, precious time. At Ziklag, David had good reason to wallow in a pit of despair. Everything he held dear was suddenly and brutally crushed. (See 1 Samuel 30:1–6.) But in that desperate moment, the habits he formed during his earlier years of spiritual training quietly assumed control of his inner man. And instead of collapsing under the pressure of discouragement as Elijah did, David looked up humbly to God and found forgiveness and a miraculously complete recovery: "And David recovered all" (vv. 18–19).

Why not follow David's example? Form now, in your days of spiritual training, the habit of spiritual resilience. Whenever you find yourself cast down, recall this vital truth: You can't afford to get down on yourself.

Chapter Four

THE SURVIVAL
OF THE FITTEST

And I will come upon him while he is weary and weak-handed, and will make him afraid…and I will smite.

—2 SAMUEL 17:2

Discouragement is not the only thing we cannot afford; spiritual weakness too will cause us to sink beneath the waves that buffet us. To overcome, we must maintain a strong spirit. The reason for this is simple: It's dog-eat-dog in this present fallen world. We either keep ourselves strong and achieve, or we sink to the bottom and fail. Everywhere we look, we see the principle of the survival of the fittest. The jungle is an especially harsh and unforgiving environment.

In the animal kingdom, the strong prey on the weak and systematically eliminate them. To continue living in the forest, animals must fight. They either win a meal or become one. It's tough, but the pressure forces them to become alert,

33

quick, wise and strong. Those who remain slow, stupid or weak don't last very long. During the millennial kingdom of Jesus Christ, the lion and the lamb will lie down together in blessed universal peace, but for the present the chase is on. The concrete jungle is another familiar killing ground.

In the business world, the competition is fierce and financially lethal. The ground rules are simple and bloody: Outsell or be outsold; put the other business under or go under yourself. One salesman's success means another's failure, always. One corporation's growth forces its rivals to downsize, merge or declare bankruptcy. This perpetual cycle of boom and bust is played out every day in every city throughout every land. Though sad, it is inevitable in this present world system, a fact of life we all take for granted. After all, business is business.

It is this very relentless commercial savagery that drives many a soul to the Savior. In the Prince of Peace the weary seek, and find, a rest and a sense of security they can find nowhere else in this rigorous, ravenous world. Because salvation is the ultimate relief, many babes in Christ mistakenly think that life *after* salvation must be thoroughly easy. So they receive Jesus into their hearts, select a local church and settle down into what they expect to be a trouble-free lifestyle. Though understandable, this concept of true Christianity is highly inaccurate. As wondrous as it is, the way of Jesus is not the "great recline." To the contrary, it is the ultimate challenge.

And so we soon discover that life in grace is yet another kind of struggle for survival—not a grappling to stay saved, but a battle to become and remain fit for the Master's use. Truly, the Christian jungle is more demanding than any other. The moment we become Christ's, the devil, a supernatural master spirit, summons all the powers and agents of his infernal region to resist us. Oswald Chambers described it as "an inspired working against." The devil cannot steal our salvation, but he can destroy our faith, ruin our fellowship with God and prevent our fruitfulness, if we fail to discern and overcome his wiles. To avoid such a capture, we must humbly learn from the overcomers of the natural jungle. Lest we become prey, we must be swift, smart and strong. Here many of us have a blind spot.

We fail to fully comprehend the viciousness of the spiritual struggle we are in. It's fierce and deadly in the spiritual jungle. Our adversary, the devil, "like a roaring lion walketh about, seeking whom he may devour" (1 Pet. 5:8). From the moment we receive Jesus into our hearts until the moment He receives us into heaven, the adversary is after us. He seeks not merely to trouble us, but to totally destroy our confidence in God. Lions don't chase their prey for sport; they kill and eat their victims: "seeking whom he may *devour*" (emphasis added). To elude our adversary and fulfill our destinies in Christ, we must be vigilant and fit at all times. Only the fittest Christians keep their faith strong and growing to the end of their earthly walk. Admittedly, many professing Christians do not understand this struggle.

Nominal churchgoers encounter no such mortal spiritual combat. The unconverted church attendee, like Cain, is religious but unregenerate. He still lives entirely in and for the things of this present world—and so serves its present prince. The same may be said of carnal Christians, born-again ones who refuse to go on to spiritual maturity or who turn back to their former sins. They too serve the enemy. Unsaved church members and carnal Christians incur no opposition from the devil. But for fully committed Christians, "disciples indeed" (John 8:31), the Bible describes life in distinctly different terms.

In almost all of its sixty-six books, the Bible portrays true saints in deadly combat with the forces of Satan. Whether examining Old or New Testament texts, the enlightened reader cannot but see the relentless and ruthless challenge every light-bearer faced from the kingdom of darkness.

Pharaoh fought to the death to prevent Israel's exodus. The Amalekites challenged Israel fiercely over the precious water they received out of the rock. Sizable Canaanite armies joined together to annihilate Joshua's forces. Herod silenced John the Baptist by decapitation. The Jewish leaders united to put Jesus on the cross. Later, they stirred deadly persecution against the growing church in Jerusalem, summarily executing Stephen without legal authorization. Paul's successful ministry in Ephesus was challenged by powerful business leaders and violent mobs. And Jesus prophesied openly that His true disciples would be betrayed, rejected and hated of all men. (See Matthew 10.) Truly, then, we cannot afford to be weak. Instinctively, our invisible arch-predator will sense his opportunity and attack.

Numerous biblical references imply, and our daily lives confirm, that Satan has an uncanny ability to sense our weak moments. When we are strong in the Lord, Satan often leaves us alone. But when by offense or sin we get out of the Spirit, he quickly detects our weakened state, and as a lion leaping to seize his prey, he strikes. The actions of Israel's diabolically inspired enemies reflect his strategy.

The Amalekites did not attack the Israelites when they were strong and thankful. But as soon as they became discouraged and weary, they quickly moved in and killed the stragglers:

> Remember what Amalek did unto thee by the way… how he met thee…and smote |those behind| thee, even all that were feeble behind thee, when thou wast faint and weary.
>
> —DEUTERONOMY 25:17–18

In the day of his betrayal, Ahithophel advised Absalom to attack King David quickly, while he was still discouraged over Absalom's coup and weakened by his flight:

And I will come upon him while he is weary and weak-handed, and will make him afraid…and I will smite the king.

—2 SAMUEL 17:2

Once when David became very weak in the heat of battle, Ishbibenob, the Philistine giant, moved quickly to slay him. Only Abishai's brave intervention saved Israel's fatigued leader from certain death.

Moreover the Philistines had yet war again with Israel; and David went down…and fought against the Philistines. And David |grew| faint. And Ishbibenob, who was of the sons of the giant…thought |of slaying| David…But Abishai, the son of Zeruiah, |came to his aid|, and smote the Philistine, and killed him.

—2 SAMUEL 21:15–17

All three of these diabolical aggressors—the Amalekites, Ahithophel and Ishbibenob—displayed the unchanging ways of our adversary. Generations come and go, but Satan's preference for attacking weak Christians remains.

This spiritual hunt knows no end in this lifetime. It's the survival of the fittest all the way through until the Lord appears: "But he that shall endure unto the end, the same shall be saved" (Matt. 24:13). Every move we make toward spiritual improvement will be challenged by the devil. He will stalk and chase us relentlessly throughout our earthly sojourn to try to take us back to our old lives. He has devoured the faith and usefulness of many before us, and he hopes to repeat his victory in our lives. It is up to us to avoid becoming yet another name on God's casualty list. To do so, we need all the help we can get.

We need to receive the baptism with the Holy Spirit to give us "power from on high" (Luke 24:49); only then may we meet our supernatural opponent on equal terms. Jesus taught plainly, "But ye shall receive power, after the Holy |Spirit| is come upon you; and ye shall be witnesses unto me" (Acts 1:8). We need to feed on God's Word daily, for only therein will we find the strength, comfort and wisdom we need daily: "Thy word is a lamp unto my feet, and a light unto my path" (Ps. 119:105). We need to pray in the Spirit frequently, for this strengthens the faith and love of God within us: "But ye, beloved, building up yourselves on your most holy faith, praying in the Holy |Spirit|, keep yourselves in the love of God" (Jude 20–21). We need the counsel of mature Christians who have gone before us in the way, for they alone, whose spiritual senses have been sharpened through successful testing, can help us discern good from evil. Instead of unequally yoking ourselves with uncommitted, insincere, Laodicean Christians, we should associate closely with serious disciples. (See 2 Corinthians 6:14–7:1.) The company we keep and the fellowship we seek inevitably influence us, either toward growth or stagnation. We need the spiritual boost afforded us by meeting regularly with our local fellowship for Bible teaching, prayer and worship at Jesus' feet. And most important, we need to heed the warning signs of personal spiritual weakness.

When our spiritual energy is low, we must examine ourselves and draw nigh the Lord for correction and refreshment. Jesus did this frequently during His earthly walk: "But He Himself would often slip away to the wilderness and pray" (Luke 5:16, NAS). In this way, we catch our weakness before it grows. Why is this so important? Because the spiritual realm is so unforgiving. A lion has no mercy for its victims. If we remain weak, our adversary will see that our weakness doesn't last long. He will lunge to disillusion us with God and drag us back, spiritually slain, to the ways of the old life. He did this to many of Jesus' original followers: "From that time many of his disciples went back, and walked no more with him" (John 6:66). And though he tried but failed to do this to the apostle Paul—"And I was delivered out of the mouth of the lion" (2 Tim. 4:17)—he succeeded in capturing and devouring one of Paul's close associates, Demas. Of this "slaying" Paul wrote sadly, "For Demas hath forsaken me, having loved this present world" (v. 10). Let us keep things in perspective.

In the kingdom of heaven, we will rest and rejoice among "harpers harping with their harps" (Rev. 14:2). But in this present world, we must watch and pray as "sheep in the midst of wolves" (Matt. 10:16). It's survival now, bliss later. For this sacred struggle, we must stay spiritually fit. Strength is the great antidote for weakness. As wise inhabitants of the spiritual jungle, we must seek strength daily. Animals know well the danger of becoming weak. Business people are careful not to let their competition get ahead of them. We too must be vigilant. Whatever it takes to keep our spirits strong—extra time with our Bibles, early rising for prayer, offerings of praise and worship, canceling unnecessary activities that drain our strength and so forth—we must do. Why? Because only the fittest disciples survive to finish the good fight and receive their crowns.

And usually they are a minority of the professing Christians of their day.

Chapter Five

LIFE IN THE
MINORITY

Or what king…is able with ten thousand to meet him
that cometh against him with twenty thousand?

—LUKE 14:31

In Luke's Gospel, Jesus described the true Christian disciple in a very brief parable. Here is His inspired story:

Or what king, going to make war against another king,
sitteth not down first, and consulteth whether he is able
with ten thousand to meet him that cometh against him
with twenty thousand? Or else, while the other is yet a
great way off, he sendeth an |embassy|, and desireth
conditions of peace. So likewise, whosoever he is of you
that forsaketh not all that he hath, cannot be my disciple.

—LUKE 14:31–33

Let's consider the symbolism He used.

41

The person who passionately follows Him, said Jesus, will be like a "king, going to make war against another king." The latter king of whom He spoke is Satan, the spiritual "prince of this world" (John 12:31). The war to which He referred is the spiritual struggle that engulfs all who seek to walk closely with God in this ungodly world. (See Matthew 10:34; 2 Timothy 3:12.) The odds in this war are most alarming. Jesus said the king going to make war was greatly outnumbered. With "ten thousand" he must go against "twenty thousand" (Luke 14:31). To succeed, therefore, Christ's disciple must have strong courage and superior strategy. Lacking either, his defeat is sure.

Paraphrasing, this is what Jesus taught us in this brief parable:

> Going on as a disciple of Mine will be like fighting in an army outnumbered two to one. If you plan to go all the way with Me, you may as well know this now: You will be in a minority in society at large and in the professing church. For one reason or another, the majority of My servants turn back and make peace with the enemy. Some become afraid, some are lazy, some surrender to the pleasures of sin, others grow bitter because of their trials and still others simply grow tired of fighting the good fight. Only a small number stand true to My Word and their calling permanently. Many start the war of discipleship, but few finish it.

In his classic allegory of the way of discipleship, *Pilgrim's Progress*, John Bunyan made the same observation about Christians. Apollyon, speaking for Satan, said:

> It is ordinary for those that have professed themselves His [Christ's] servants after awhile to give Him the slip and return again to me.

Both Christ's infallible parable and Bunyan's inspired

dream echo the great keynote Christ sounded in His Sermon on the Mount:

> Enter in at the |narrow| gate; for wide is the gate, and broad is the way, that leadeth to destruction, and *many* there be who go in that way; because |narrow| is the gate, and |hard| is the way, which leadeth unto life, and…*few* there be that find it.
>
> —MATTHEW 7:13–14, EMPHASIS ADDED

Jesus prophesied here that "many" who profess Him will choose the broad, easy way of carnal Christianity, which leads ultimately to the destruction of their usefulness to God. Only the "few" will submit themselves to the difficult, yet rewarding disciplines of the narrow way and become abiding, fruitful branches in the vine of God. Any honest appraisal of Christianity today will confirm these findings.

The true disciple, like the king going to make war, usually finds himself outnumbered in his earthly conflicts. Rarely will he be found in full agreement with the majority opinion in matters of spiritual or moral controversy. Why? Because the king with whom he battles, Satan, holds the unbelieving majority of the inhabitants of this world in spiritual and psychological subjection. The unsaved are of his spirit and nature: "Ye are of your father the devil" (John 8:44). Therefore, the satanic majority thinks like him, acts like him and sides with him: "And the lusts of your father ye will do" (v. 44). This leaves God's children always at a numerical disadvantage. It is for this reason that Scripture refers to God's faithful ones as His "remnant": "Though the number of the children of Israel be as the sand of the sea, a *remnant* shall be saved" (Rom. 9:27, emphasis added). A *remnant* is "a small number of people remaining from a larger, original group." Consider these biblical examples of righteous remnants.

THE FAITHFUL ISRAELITES IN ELIJAH'S DAY

God informed Elijah that there were seven thousand faithful souls in Israel in his day: "Yet I have left me seven thousand in Israel, all the knees which have not bowed unto Baal" (1 Kings 19:18). That sounds like a large number, but we must remember that there were *millions* of Israelites living at the time. In comparison, then, the seven thousand were but a few.

THE TRUE PROPHETS IN ISRAEL

During much of the period of Israel's monarchy, especially its latter years, her true prophets were usually outnumbered by her false prophets. Elijah withstood four hundred and fifty false prophets on Mount Carmel. Micaiah's messages often contradicted four hundred false prophetic voices in Samaria (1 Kings 22:6–8). For years Ezekiel's was a lone voice of truth amid those prophesying to the Jews in Babylon. Jeremiah stood alone against all Jerusalem, its king and its princes while his fellow prophets mocked and persecuted him. In these cases, and many others, only a small handful of faithful Israelites stood by the true prophets. The majority of Jews supported the false prophets and the evil leaders they flattered.

ISRAEL'S ARMIES

Israel's armies were often greatly outnumbered by their foes. The very first war recorded in Scripture pitted Abraham and his "three hundred and eighteen" servants against the much larger army of Chedorlaomer. (See Genesis 14:13–16.) It was indeed a case of meeting "twenty thousand with ten thousand," and it set the standard for most of Israel's conflicts that followed. Numerically, the odds were stacked against the Hebrew warriors nearly every time they drew their swords. Gideon and his three hundred attacked hordes of Midianites; King Asa's thousands faced a million Ethiopians; King

Hezekiah's forces were besieged by Sennacherib's innumerable host. But always in these clashes, God and His righteous minority prevailed.

THE APOSTLES

No matter how many times and ways He counted them, Jesus' apostles numbered only twelve. Thus, in its embryonic period, the Way had a decidedly smaller membership than the other Jewish "denominations" of Jesus' day—the Pharisees and the Sadducees. Yet Jesus' little remnant was built on the immovable twin pillars of truth and right. When envy drove the larger Jewish bodies to try to stamp out the rival movement by killing the Nazarene and scattering His followers, despite the weight of their prestige, tradition, wealth and greater numbers, they failed. Jesus' righteous minority survived. Then it blossomed and transformed the world.

To this day the principle of the remnant is still operable. Fully committed disciples, Christians who are uncompromisingly loyal to Jesus, are greatly outnumbered by carnal Christians and the unsaved masses. God's faithful remnant is a veritable Gideon's army against a whole world of Midianites. One reason for this is that the professing church today suffers from powerful gusts of faddism. Failing to hoist her sails to the full, steady winds of Bible truth, the good ship Christendom has instead been driven to and fro upon the sea of life by every unstable wind of doctrine devised by crafty men for their gain and her harm. Consequently, certain trends are popular for a time, then die out. We are infatuated with one craze, then another. In the midst of Christianity's popular drift, the discerning disciple must remember this: If left to itself, the body of Christ does not always know what is best for itself.

A Revelation: The Majority Is Not Always Right

Israel's congregation certainly did not always make the right choices. At Sinai, to a man the Israelites asked *not* to hear God's voice any more; they preferred to hear only Moses. When Moses tarried on Mount Sinai, the people quickly united to build a golden calf and worship it. At Kadesh-barnea, Israel's electorate voted overwhelmingly *not* to trust God and invade Canaan. And during long stretches of Israel's monarchy, idolatry, particularly the worship of Baal, was the religion of choice for the majority of the Jews. Only when righteous kings arose did reformation and revival produce the phenomenon of a righteous majority among the children of Israel. Sadly, modern Christianity has largely failed to learn from the example of Israel's unspiritual majority.

Our Laodicean majority also suffers poor spiritual judgment. Our most popular religious leaders sometimes do not lead us in the right direction. Our bestsellers are not always the best books. Our most popular projects and activities sometimes have little spiritual value. Too often our prevailing doctrines are not "what the Spirit saith unto the churches." Consequently, the going thing is usually not the right thing. One reason for this spiritual misdirection is that most believers suffer from "herd mentality"—the inclination to trust blindly in the wisdom of the majority, to go with the crowd, to assume that the greatest number must be right in all decisions. This persistent fallacy is a great hindrance to true discipleship, for Christ's true learners must often take the less-traveled way, yet they are fully right in doing so. Why can't we see this?

One reason for our blurred vision is the prevalence of democracy. Democracy is the best system of *human* government to appear in the history of the world, bar none. Every other conceivable system of rule—monarchism, totalitarianism, fascism, socialism, communism, even anarchy!—has

46

entered the world's stage only to be eventually booed off as unacceptable. But democracy lives on. It is undoubtedly the fairest method of governing this presently unfair world. Yet here is our blind spot: Democratic rule, though desirable, is not divine. Majority rule, though fair, is not infallible. The majority may be right, but they may also err tragically. Only God's judgment is always right. Hence the spiritual and moral principles of His Word alone cannot lead astray: "For the word of the LORD is right" (Ps. 33:4). The wise Christian, realizing this, always takes positions that are aligned with the teachings or principles of the Bible, whether that places him in the majority or minority of his peers. The spiritually blind Christian, however, always shifts his position to agree with the greater number, believing that therein lies safety. Besides, human pride finds it very uncomfortable to confess and maintain a minority opinion. The Christian that lives by this "poll guidance" puts himself off of the narrow way that leads to full spiritual life and fruitfulness. Why do the unspiritual masses—Christian and non-Christian—fail to recognize what is best for themselves in many spiritually and morally related issues?

In a word, that reason is sin. Sin—rebellion against God's revealed will—blinds the sinner both spiritually and morally. It is impossible to habitually practice sin and retain clear moral vision; one or the other will be surrendered. By forsaking God, Adam's children have lost touch with the lone source of eternal wisdom. Consequently, every Christ-rejecting generation manifests an ever-increasing loss of good judgment in moral and spiritual matters. The will of the sinful majority grows ever more unhealthy and self-destructive as time passes. Only genuinely heaven-sent revival breaks this disturbing downward spiral. How many times has history proven these facts?

Today in America, the majority of voters have elected the various leaders who over the last long generation have led us straight into a sinkhole of moral confusion and social chaos.

Amoral trends and policies have virtually produced a new and sadly fallen American national character, a society in which unjustified divorce is rampant, abortion is constant, AIDS is spreading, illegal drugs are ubiquitous, our public schools are war zones, and terrorism threatens almost every phase of our daily lives. If the majority and its core of chosen leaders are indeed pursuing the course that is best for us, why is our society—particularly its most basic and mandatory institutions of marriage and family—falling apart all around us? Because as a society rife with practicing sinners, our collective good judgment has gone from us. In many key moral issues—abortion, homosexuality, pornography, crime-glorifying rap music, gun control and so forth—an ominously large and growing number of Americans no longer recognize, or even care, what is best for the nation as a whole.

The real problem for disciples, however, is not the manifold social ills of this or any other nation. It is the spiritual condition of the majority of professing *Christians* in this terminal, Laodicean period of the church age. (See Revelation 3:15–17.) Today most Christians are not fully conformed to biblical standards. Only in certain areas of living and ministering do we and our churches walk in the ways of God. In many matters we just quietly conform ourselves to the ways of our culture or the fads of popular Christianity, whether biblical or not. This silent sellout puts every determined disciple on the spot. Will he conform to his Laodicean peers, or will he be "transformed" (Rom. 12:2)? Will he walk in the light of the Word, or will he just fall in with the religious majority, no questions asked? To be uncompromisingly loyal to Jesus Christ, to truly keep the Word of His patience, the disciple will have to go "|outside| the camp, bearing his reproach" (Heb. 13:13) at least once, maybe more, during his Christian walk, as did our Lord, the prophets, the martyrs and all the reformers and revivalists of the church age. This will involve making correct but unpopular choices and taking the consequences of those choices. That will mean bearing the cross or, more specifically, accepting life in the ecclesiastical minority—at least, until biblical revival comes.

A COUNTER-REVELATION: THE MINORITY IS NOT ALWAYS RIGHT EITHER!

If he is humble and sensitive to God, the developing disciple will also avoid the trap of blind opposition. By blind opposition we mean taking the side *opposite* the majority in every controversy, assuming that always to be God's side. This idea that the minority is always right is another fraud that must be exposed. In the Book of Proverbs, God warns us against being led purely by our own calculations: "Lean not unto thine own understanding" (Prov. 3:5). In this matter, as in many others, our logic is deficient. Although the opinions of the Laodicean majority often err spiritually, that does not mean they are always wrong. So beware of the swing of your cerebral pendulum. Never choose the unpopular opinion merely because it is unpopular. Choose rather what the statements and principles of the Word of God advocate, as best you see it, whether few or many support that position.

~

Don't be discouraged, my friend. There *is* a kingdom where the children of truth will always be in the majority. But we shall not experience that blessed theocracy until the awesome clash of Armageddon has purged this present world system and its antichrist majority. In that new day the righteous will pervade every city, nation and continent. Truly, "the meek shall inherit the earth, and shall delight themselves in the abundance of peace" (Ps. 37:11).

But until then, faithful Christian disciples are like kings going to battle against a more numerous foe. God's decree, at present, is life in the minority.

49

Chapter Six

WHEN EVERYTHING
IS UPSIDE DOWN

Then Abimelech called Abraham, and said unto him,
What hast thou done unto us?

—GENESIS 20:9

To help us enjoy life in the minority, rising above every
wave that befalls us there, God has given us many
invaluable spiritual gifts, including the life of Jesus, the Holy
Spirit, the gifts of the Spirit and gifted ministers. James confirms that these, and all other good gifts, come from God:
"Every good gift and every perfect gift is from above...from
the Father" (James 1:17). But thanks to Adam's rebellion,
human beings are born with certain other gifts, or abilities,
that are clearly not good and cannot be said to have origi-
nated with the Father. One of these is the gift of stupidity—
an innate knack for fouling things up all by ourselves!

We know well of this gift's operation in certain prominent Bible characters. Samson, Jacob and Jonah excelled at creating large and confusing problems for themselves and others. Why, even the holy apostles demonstrated this gift on a few occasions—rebuking Jesus for announcing His intention to go to the cross, calling down fire on the Samaritans, murmuring against Mary of Bethany for anointing Jesus and disputing among themselves who should be the greatest. But the twentieth chapter of Genesis packs an even greater surprise. There we find the gift of stupidity working in one whom we would expect to be without it, namely Abraham. Yes, Abraham, the first called to the life of faith; Abraham, the father of Israel; Abraham, the spiritual forerunner of every Christian. Even he managed to create an entangled mess at Gerar. It happened on this wise.

Shortly after the cataclysmic judgment of Sodom in Genesis 19, Abraham changed his residence, for what reason we do not know. (See Genesis 20:1.) Perhaps he found life in the vicinity of such a desolate disaster zone a bit too unpleasant. Whatever his reasons, down to Gerar he went—with neither orders nor permission from on high. Once relocated, the chosen patriarch was visited by a very wrong thought, one he had not entertained for over twenty years: It came to his heart to lie about Sarah's identity lest his Philistine neighbors should kill him to take her as a wife. Make no mistake: This was the stupidity of Abraham, not the faith of Abraham, in operation. When Abraham said of Sarah, "She is my sister" (Gen. 20:2), Abimelech, king of Gerar, obviously attracted to her, promptly took Abraham's "sibling" into his royal harem. By forging a lie to protect himself, Abraham turned aside from his usual uprightness and faith in God. It was a change of heart he would soon regret.

The day Abraham turned aside, God turned his world upside down. Because he had departed from God's way, God disrupted his way. (See chapter 1, pages 3–5.) A circus of upside-down events followed, each ring of which contained something precisely the opposite of what it should have been. Consider how out of place, how topsy-turvy, Abraham's circumstances were as long as this man of light walked in the paths of darkness.

THE RIGHTEOUS ACT WRONGLY AND THE UNRIGHTEOUS ACT RIGHTLY

Having been previously justified by faith (Gen. 15:6), Abraham was a man right with God in the day he entered Gerar. Abimelech, however, an idol-worshiping Philistine king, was not.

Yet in this inverted instance, Abraham, who was righteous, wronged Abimelech, who was unrighteous. Scripture reveals that Abraham's deliberately incomplete description of Sarah caused Abimelech to trespass. Abimelech took another man's wife into his harem only because he believed Abraham's false story—that Sarah was merely his sister and hence unmarried. God Himself confirmed this. When Abimelech protested, "In the integrity of my heart…have I done this," God responded, "Yea, I know that thou didst this in the integrity of thy heart…" (Gen. 20:5–6).

This divine admission proves clearly that, on this odd occasion, the righteous acted wrongly and the unrighteous acted rightly. It was a case of a justified man acting less justly than an unjustified man. Incredibly, Abraham was the fraud and Abimelech the defrauded.

THE WISE FEAR MEN AND THE FOOLISH FEAR GOD

In the Bible, wisdom and the fear of the Lord are synonymous. Where one is, there is always the other: "The fear of the LORD is the beginning of wisdom" (Prov. 9:10). Knowing Abraham to be one of the wisest of men, we would expect him always to fear God. Moreover, the Bible equates unbelief with folly. No matter how high one's intelligence quotient, he is a fool who denies the existence of God: "The fool hath said in his heart, There is no God" (Ps. 53:1). Since Abimelech was an unbeliever, and hence a foolish man, we would expect him not to fear God. But in keeping with the rest of this story, just the opposite occurred in Gerar: The fool feared God, while the wise man feared men.

By leaning to his own understanding, Abraham's heart was pierced by the fiery darts of the fear of man: "And Abraham said…Surely the fear of God is not in this place; and they [the men of Gerar] will slay me for my wife's sake" (Gen. 20:11). It was this reasonable fear that moved him to forge a lie for his own self-protection. But his blanket judgment of the Philistines ("the fear of God is not in this place") soon proved to be quite wrong. When God warned Abimelech of his error in a dream by night, the Philistine ruler manifested an extraordinary fear of God. He obeyed immediately, rising early the next morning to inform his servants (v. 8), converse with Abraham (vv. 9–13), restore Sarah, give Abraham gifts (vv. 14–16) and send him away, blessings in tow.

THE CHILDREN OF TRUTH LIE AND THE CHILDREN OF A LIE SPEAK THE TRUTH

In no way were Abraham and Sarah deceived by the false glory of the Philistine idols. They believed firmly in the true and living God who had called them from Ur and had kept and blessed them in the way. Because they thus knew the Truth, they spoke and walked in the truth consistently. In every respect, then, Abraham and Sarah were children of truth.

Abimelech and his servants, however, were the children of a lie. Unacquainted with the Truth and convinced that their idols were real, the Philistines lived in the darkness of religious error. Because of these vastly different spiritual perspectives, in any given dispute we would expect Abraham's household to tell the truth and the people of Abimelech to lie.

But in this dispute things didn't work out that way. Uncharacteristically, Abraham and Sarah conspired to sell falsehood. Indeed, Abraham did not act alone in his crime against the house of Abimelech; Sarah was his willing and active accomplice. When Abraham said, "She is my sister" (Gen. 20:2), Sarah promptly confirmed his story in her own words. Abimelech later protested that they both had misled him: "Said he not unto me, she is my sister? And she, even she herself said, He is my brother" (v. 5; see verse 13). Meanwhile, Abimelech and the members of his household behaved as genuine children of truth. They told not the first lie, either to man or God. It was yet another paradox: The children of truth lied, and the children of a lie spoke the truth.

THE PROPHET IS PASSED BY
AND THE HEATHEN HEAR FROM HEAVEN

During His visitation God informed Abimelech that Abraham was a prophet: "Restore the man [Abraham] his wife; for he is a prophet" (Gen. 20:7). As such, Abraham was a sensitive soul, keenly attuned to heavenly frequencies and accustomed to receiving divine transmissions regularly. But because of his disobedience regarding Sarah's identity, Abraham heard nothing from heaven while in Gerar. His remarkably powerful spiritual communications system was temporarily shut down. Meanwhile Abimelech, an unspiritual man of the world, received a heavenly communiqué. God spoke to him as if he were the prophet, not Abraham, in a dream of the night: "But God came to Abimelech in a dream by night, and said..." (v. 3). Yet Abimelech was no seer. Prophets are redeemed ones who, among other things, are divinely appointed to receive heavenly visions: "If there be a prophet among you, I the LORD will make myself known unto him in a vision, and will speak unto him in a dream" (Num. 12:6). And, typically, worldlings such as Abimelech have no ears to hear what the Spirit is saying. But remember, in Gerar nothing was typical.

There the prophet was passed by and the heathen heard from heaven. Abraham's spiritual radio was silent, while Abimelech's buzzed with the word of the Lord.

THE CORRECTOR IS CORRECTED
BY THE SINNER

God normally uses prophets as His agents of correction. By rebukes, warnings and pleadings, they attempt to sway the deceived to forsake their errors and return to the Lord and the way of life. (See 2 Samuel 12:1–14.) But like those previously cited, this norm too was reversed in Gerar. There God used Abimelech, a sinner, to correct Abraham, a prophet.

And Abimelech performed surprisingly well. He took the man of God to task with holy boldness, humbling him with embarrassingly sharp questions, indefensible allegations and rebukes: "Then Abimelech called Abraham, and said unto him, What hast thou done unto us? And what have I offended thee, that thou hast brought on me and on my kingdom a great sin? Thou hast done deeds unto me that ought not to be done…What Ididst thou have in viewI, that thou hast done this thing?" (Gen. 20:9–10). Thus Abraham, the corrector, stood corrected.

THE VICTIM MAKES RESTITUTION
TO THE CRIMINAL

When the case of Abraham vs. Abimelech went to trial, Abimelech was the plaintiff and Abraham the defendant. After hearing the evidence, the Judge of all the earth declared the predictable verdict: Abraham was guilty as charged! But His sentence caught everyone by surprise.

Abimelech, not Abraham, was ordered to make restitution: "Now therefore restore the man his wife" (Gen. 20:7). Plus God sternly warned Abimelech that the penalty for non-compliance was death: "And if thou restore her not, know thou that thou shalt surely die, thou, and all that are thine." Incredibly, the Judge required nothing of Abraham but a confession. This was most remarkable, for when Abimelech took Sarah into his harem he undoubtedly compensated Abraham for the hand of his "sister." (See Genesis 12:15–16.) Yet Abraham was not ordered to restore these gifts, nor was he stiffly warned with the threat of death. Abimelech's response, too, must have taken Abraham by surprise.

Abimelech went far beyond what was required of him. After restoring Sarah, he gave Abraham many additional gifts and benefits. He gave him animals and servants: "And Abimelech took sheep, and oxen, and menservants, and womenservants, and gave them unto Abraham" (Gen. 20:14). He enriched him with a thousand pieces of silver: "And unto Sarah he [Abimelech] said, Behold, I have given thy brother a thousand pieces of silver" (v. 16). And he graciously invited Abraham to sojourn in the best of his land without charge: "And Abimelech said, Behold, my land is before thee: dwell where it pleaseth thee" (v. 15). So the troubled one compensated his troubler, who benefited immensely from the whole affair.

The case set an undeniably strange precedent: The victim made restitution to the criminal. Philistia's court watchers must have left scratching their heads.

The Innocent Healed by the Prayer of the Guilty

It is the biblical rule for guilty sinners to be forgiven and/or healed by the prayers of the righteous. (See James 5:14–15.) For instance, when God had heard enough of the false accusations and cruel condemnations Job's three friends heaped upon him, He ordered them to repent by going to Job for

57

prayer. (See Job 42:7–9.) When they obeyed, they received forgiveness and restoration with God by means of Job's intercession. Also, after Miriam was stricken with leprosy for murmuring against Moses, she was healed by Moses' urgent prayer. (See Numbers 12:13.) In both of these examples, the guilty were restored by the prayers of the innocent.

But in Gerar the exception to this rule manifested. Before leaving town, Abraham prayed for Abimelech and his entire household, whom God had stricken with infertility: "So Abraham prayed unto God" (Gen. 20:17). And God graciously answered, healing everyone affected: "And God healed Abimelech, and his wife, and his maidservants." So this story produced one final funny twist: The family of the innocent was healed by the prayer of the guilty.

～

As soon as Abraham confessed his sin and returned to his uprightness, God turned his world right side up again and put him back on track for glory. Good things followed very quickly. Isaac, the long-awaited son of promise, was born. (See Genesis 21:1–8.) And suddenly, the fear and shame of Gerar were eclipsed by the laughter and joy of a divine fulfillment. What does all this mean to you?

Well, let me ask, Do your present circumstances in any way resemble those of Abraham in Gerar? Is *your* life turned upside down? Granted, such confusing scenarios sometimes besiege those who are perfectly upright. That's the message of the Book of Job. But in many cases, the gift of stupidity is the culprit. And if so, you'll find that it's impossible to walk calmly on stormy waters if you are churning them daily by your stubborn refusal to obey the voice of the Lord. Abraham couldn't do so—nor could Peter, or any other redeemed mortal, for that matter! Honest self-examination is always in order.

If after humble retrospection you realize you have indeed

caused your current problem, don't let discouragement trouble you further. Remember instead that even the wise can create foolish messes occasionally if they fail to abide, trust and obey. Abraham did. That's the primary message of the twentieth chapter of the Book of Genesis. Then get to the root of your confusion and root it out, that God may halt your merry-go-round of trouble and let you off and restore you to the paths of glory. There good things—fulfillments, blessings, deliverances—will shortly come your way. That's the rest of the message. Provided, of course, that we obey the Lord willingly.

Chapter Seven

"WILLINGLY"

Then they willingly received him into the |boat|; and immediately the |boat| was at the land to which they went.

—JOHN 6:21

It is amazing how quickly God delivers us from some trials when we obey Him with a willing spirit. The disciples' second-recorded crossing of the Sea of Galilee demonstrates this. (See John 6:15–21.)

After rowing for hours on the dark, storming Sea of Galilee, Jesus' weary disciples spotted a mysterious figure "walking on the sea, and drawing |near| unto the |boat|" (John 6:19). Terrified and unaware that the apparition was actually their Master, "they were afraid" (v. 19) and quite unwilling to receive whoever or whatever it was into their boat. (See Mark 6:49–50.) Sensing their terror, Jesus quickly identified Himself: "It is I; be not afraid" (John 6:20). The disciples then changed their minds and "willingly received him into the |boat|" (v. 21). "Immediately," or that very moment, their harrowing trial ended: "And *immediately* the |boat| was at the land to which they went" (v. 21, emphasis added). And to their surprise, all conditions were suddenly back to normal. After disembarking, they stood again on solid ground, safe from the perilous waters. They were in the plains of Gennesaret, near their desired destination of Capernaum. And most importantly, Jesus was present with them as before. The immediacy of their deliverance was more than a coincidence.

Indeed the sum of the evidence given us by the four Gospel writers indicates that the disciples' sudden landfall was yet another stunning miracle of Christ. Consider these facts.

THE FACTS

We know that the disciples embarked on their stormy voyage near the site where Jesus fed the five thousand. (See John 6:5–14.) Luke's Gospel reveals that this was a deserted place on the eastern shore of Galilee near, and apparently just south of, the city of Bethsaida. (See Luke 9:10.) (Please refer to a map of the areas surrounding the Sea of Galilee during this period.) John revealed that their intended destination was Capernaum (John 6:17), the city in which Jesus' ministry was based. But apparently the violence of the storm blew the disciples' harried vessel off course, sending them on a more southerly course than they had plotted. Capernaum was only a short distance from their departure point, about three to four miles due west. Yet after they had rowed this distance (John 6:19), they were still tossed about in the storm, apparently well south of Capernaum. It was then that Jesus appeared, they received him willingly into their boat, and "immediately" they found themselves at the lake's edge—only this shoreline was by the plain of Gennesaret, not

Capernaum, as they had hoped. (See Matthew 14:34; Mark 6:53.) They then completed their trip by disembarking and walking north to Capernaum, where they were met by the anxious crowds Jesus had fed the day before near Bethsaida (John 6:24–25).

While the other Gospel writers who described this incident remained silent on this point, John drew attention to the fact that after the disciples received Jesus into their boat, they arrived at the shore "immediately." This implies that their voyage was miraculously shortened. That can mean only one thing: By His supernatural power the Holy Spirit transported their boat across the waters in a moment of time, just as He later transported Philip, the evangelist, bodily from the Gaza desert to Azotus. (See Acts 8:39–40.) The original language used helps us determine this.

In John 6:21, "immediately" is the rendering the King James Version translators gave the Greek word *eutheos*, which means "at once." By inspiration, the apostle John used the same Greek word earlier in his Gospel when describing the healing of the impotent man by the pool of Bethesda: "And immediately [*eutheos*] the man was made |well|, and took up his bed, and walked" (John 5:9). We know this usage described an instantaneous miracle, not a gradual occurrence. Hence, we may assume that, by using *eutheos* to describe the disciples' sudden landfall, John's intention was precisely the same. In both contexts, he purposely selected this word to describe something that occurred in a moment and not over time. (Note that the Holy Spirit also prompted the use of *eutheos* when John recorded his own Rapture-like experience on the Isle of Patmos [Rev. 4:2] and when Luke recorded the instantaneous healings of Saul of Tarsus and Aeneas [Acts 9:18, 34].)

In addition, several excellent translations of the New Testament use language that supports the conclusion that a miraculous transportation occurred:

And *at once* the boat reached the shore they were making for.

—JOHN 6:21, PHILLIPS, EMPHASIS ADDED

And now the boat went *at once* to the land they steered for—and *immediately* they reached the shore toward which they had been [slowly] making.

—JOHN 6:21, AMP, EMPHASIS ADDED

And *in a moment* the boat reached the shore at the point to which they were going.

—JOHN 6:21, WEYMOUTH, EMPHASIS ADDED

To deny that a supernatural passage occurred—whether two hundred yards or two miles—is to deny the obvious. Consider these additional points:

- If the disciples' boat were already near the land when Jesus appeared, why did He not stand and call to them from the shore, as He did later in a similar situation? (See John 21:4–8.) There would be no need for Him to walk across the water to meet them if they were already very close to land. Obviously, they were still in deep waters.

- Why did the Holy Spirit inspire John to note the distance they had traveled at the time they sighted Jesus? "They had rowed about five and twenty or thirty furlongs [three to four miles]" (John 6:19). Why did He not rather prompt John to write, "When they drew near the shore," if no miracle occurred? It seems obvious that the Holy Spirit mentioned the distance traveled so the reader would realize that the disciples were blown off course by the storm. Normally, after rowing three to four miles due west they would have made landfall at Capernaum. That they had not indicates they were

64

off course at the time, probably still being driven south by the prevailing winds toward the churning center of Lake Galilee and in desperate need of help. Hence, Christ's miraculous intervention.

Understanding the symbolism in this incident will enable us to grasp the spirit of the Word—the life-giving message the Spirit is sending to every sorely tried Christian.

THE SYMBOLISM

The symbolism is as follows: Jesus is, and therefore represents, *the Word of God.* The boat, the setting in which the disciples were held and tested, represents our *trying circumstances.* The raging storm, which pressed against the disciples so persistently, represents the *relentless pressure* of our trials of faith. The disciples' act of willingly receiving Jesus into their boat represents the tried believer *yielding to God's Word and obeying it willingly in the midst of his trying circumstances.* And the land, where the disciples found relief, represents *the ends of our trials* or our *deliverance points*—the times and places at which we are released to return to normal circumstances. Let's focus on the turning point of this story.

While afraid and unsure of Jesus' identity, the disciples refused to receive Him into their boat; thus, they rejected Him. As long as this rejection continued, they remained buffeted and afflicted, without a "way to escape" (1 Cor. 10:13). But the moment they changed their attitudes and received Jesus, and that "willingly," their circumstances changed dramatically. They escaped the storm's hindering grip and "immediately" reached land.

THE SPIRIT OF THE WORD

Here is the Spirit's message to believers. If when harried by the pressure of our trials we seek God's way of escape, there is but one way to get it: We must obey God willingly. If we reject His will (His Word or the leading of His Spirit), as the disciples initially rejected Jesus, we abide in a state of well-deserved misery. If we surrender and obey, we will be transported to our deliverance point. That is, at once we will be internally liberated by God's Spirit and externally helped by His hand.

However, there are two conditions for this scenario: Our obedience must be the right kind, and our trial must be one that may be terminated by obedience alone.

Two Kinds of Obedience

Not all obedience is the same. Sometimes we obey grudgingly; we are obedient in act but still resistant in spirit. At other times we obey willingly; we are obedient in act and surrendered in spirit. This willing obedience is always accompanied by a sense of inner freedom and delight. Grudging obedience, however, is marked by tightness, a sense of straining and an absence of joy. God wants every believer to be clothed with the mantle of willing obedience.

When He deals with us to "put on" (Col. 3:10, 12) willing obedience to His Word, He does so in a specific way. Through devotional reading, biblical instruction or pastoral counsel, the Spirit of God impresses our hearts with a verse, passage or principle of Scripture. Why? Because He wants us to incorporate it into our way of life. Soon afterward He arranges circumstances in which to try us, to see if we will humble ourselves and work out our own salvation by actually doing the thing of which He has spoken. Being holy, He will accept nothing less than our full obedience; we must freely comply on the exact point He is dealing with us about. This is the idea Mary conveyed to the servants in Cana when she said, "Whatsoever he saith unto you, do it" (John 2:5). If in the midst of our stormy trials we refuse to willingly obey the Words and ways that God is compelling us to put on, we abide clothed in the ugly sackcloth of stubbornness. And we make our hard trials even harder.

How hard it was when the disciples, beset by buffetings and perils, refused to let Jesus into their troubled little boat! And how hard it is when we foolishly try to find deliverance from our stormy trials without obeying God's will! Invariably, we find ourselves in the position the disciples were in—in darkness, vexed by repeated blows of trouble, tossed and tormented with fear, bone weary and desperate for a way of escape. As long as we refuse to yield on the point of obedience the Lord seeks, we remain locked into our tempestuous situation. And because pride and stubbornness prevail within us, God Himself joins with the forces of the air to resist us, for "God resisteth the proud" (James 4:6). But the moment we humble ourselves and obey willingly, He graciously gives us deliverance, for "God…giveth grace unto the humble" (v. 6).

It is therefore clear that, in evaluating our obedience, the Lord takes more into account than our outward compliance with His will. He looks beyond our acts to our spirit, our true heart attitude: "The LORD looketh on the heart" (1 Sam. 16:7). While observing us, He asks this question: Of what spirit is our obedience? Do we carry out His will gladly or somberly? Is a pure stream of joy or the venom of suppressed anger flowing through our hearts as we comply? Are we free in spirit or bound up? Single-minded or double-minded? Such will determine if our obedience is the kind He approves.

"Study to show thyself approved unto God" (2 Tim. 2:15). God reserves His approval for those who serve Him willingly, in the pure delight of wholehearted surrender. The disciples eventually gave Him such in the midst of the raging storm: "Then they were *quite willing and glad* for Him to come into the boat" (John 6:21, AMP, emphasis added). Throughout Scripture the Spirit praises, and so recommends to every reader, willing obedience to God. Consider these references:

I *delight* to do thy will, O my God.
—PSALM 40:8, EMPHASIS ADDED

And whatever ye do, do it *heartily*, as to the Lord, and not unto men, knowing that of the Lord ye shall receive the reward of the inheritance.
—COLOSSIANS 3:23–24, EMPHASIS ADDED

Most gladly, therefore, will I rather glory in my infirmities...Therefore, I take *pleasure* in...
—2 CORINTHIANS 12:9–10, EMPHASIS ADDED

God loveth a *cheerful* giver.
—2 CORINTHIANS 9:7, EMPHASIS ADDED

Serve him with a perfect heart and with a *willing* mind; for the LORD searcheth all hearts, and understandeth all the imaginations of the thoughts.
—1 CHRONICLES 28:9, EMPHASIS ADDED

If ye be *willing* and obedient, ye shall eat the good of the land.
—ISAIAH 1:19, EMPHASIS ADDED

Feed the flock of God which is among you, taking the oversight of it, not by constraint but *willingly*; not for filthy lucre but of a ready mind.
—1 PETER 5:2, EMPHASIS ADDED

For if I do this thing *willingly*, I have a reward.
—1 CORINTHIANS 9:17, EMPHASIS ADDED

David consistently served God with a willing spirit. When Abigail warned him not to take vengeance on Nabal, but rather to leave place for God's wrath, David recognized that God was speaking to him. (See 1 Samuel 25.) Hence, despite his present heat of anger, he yielded and promptly turned back. But unlike many of smaller character, David obeyed willingly. There was no, "I wish I didn't have to do this," suppressed in his heart. He gladly committed Nabal to God and went his way without a trace of resentment. For this reason God intervened immediately, ending David's storm of reproach: "About ten days after...the LORD smote Nabal, that he died" (1 Sam. 25:38). God's intervention confirmed His approval of David's obedience. But He doesn't approve of those who merely go through the motions of obedience while nursing rebellion in their hearts. The Bible gives us many examples of this unworthy obedience.

For instance, when Moses urgently ordered Zipporah to circumcise their second son, Zipporah complied, but her rude language and actions betrayed a heart that hated having to obey God's will. (See Exodus 4:24–26.) When King Ahasuerus asked Haman to honor Mordecai with a citywide parade, Haman obeyed, but he was mortified with shame and rage the entire time. (See Esther 6:10–13.) When Laban finally overtook his fleeing son-in-law, Jacob, he obeyed God's command not to harm him, but his hostile words and actions reveal that he still *wanted* to: "It is in the power of my hand to do you |harm|; but the God of your father spoke unto me |last night|" (Gen. 31:29; see verses 25–55). Zipporah, Haman, Laban—hilarious obeyers they were not! And as such, their obedience was not the kind God approves.

THE FACTORS THAT DETERMINE
WHEN OUR TRIALS END

Our Christian trials do not end haphazardly. Our heavenly Father personally terminates them based chiefly upon two factors—our willing obedience and His appointed times.

Our willing obedience

God orders some trials solely to bend our stiff wills in issues where previously we have consistently resisted Him. He providentially creates circumstances more turbulent than any we have faced before, hoping the increased pressure will provoke us to a new and lasting surrender of will in that issue. If we remain stubborn, our trial continues. If we obey with a broken and contrite spirit, the Lord quickly releases us from our trying circumstances, as He did the apostles.

God's appointed times

Some trials continue for a season even after we have obeyed God willingly. Why? Because the Lord has appointed a time for our trial to end: "For the vision is yet for an appointed time, but at the end it shall speak, and not lie" (Hab. 2:3). (See also Psalm 102:13.) From the beginning He has used His hourglass to terminate times of testing.

God determined that the Israelites would not leave Egypt until four hundred years had expired. (See Genesis 15:13–14.) He set the year and season of Isaac's birth, which ended Abraham's long trial of faith. (See Genesis 17:21; 21:2.) He decided that Joseph's imprisonment would not end until the time came to prepare for the worldwide famine. (See Psalm 105:19.) He decreed the Jews' Babylonian captivity would last seventy years. (See Jeremiah 29:10.) He determined that Jesus' trial of death would not end until the third day. (See Matthew 16:21.) And He appointed three and a half years as the duration of Israel's Great Tribulation yet to come. (See Daniel 7:21–22, 25–26; Revelation 12:14.) Regardless of the willing obedience of His people, the lengths of these trials were divinely set and hence unchangeable.

Why does God set appointed times to deliver us? Because:

1. The Lord is developing the fruit of the Spirit in our souls. The passage of time is a necessary part of the ripening process. Accordingly, how can the fruit of the Spirit (Gal. 5:22–23)—especially long-suffering, patience, faith and self-control—be developed in us if every trial ends the moment we obey God joyfully?

2. The Lord is perfecting our skills, such as organization, management, problem-solving, handling difficult people, counseling, ministry gifts and so on. Only practice makes perfect. How, then, can we perfect our skills unless lengthy tests afford us plenty of time and opportunities to practice them?

3. The Lord is establishing our characters. After clay pots are fully formed they are fired; into the furnace they go until the potter's appointed time of release. Accordingly, after Christ's character has been adequately shaped in us through many acts of trust and obedience, God constrains us to endure protracted trials merely to "fire" us. Then our characters (habitual actions in, and reactions to, life) become "permanentized" and predictably faithful, like our Lord's. Therefore, God can entrust us with greater tasks in this life and the next.

4. The Lord is working our circumstances together with those of other believers so that jointly we may reach a good and joyful end. We may have to wait out a trial while others learn the ways and graces of God we have already perfected. Joshua and Caleb endured wilderness hardships for many years while the faith of Israel's younger generation rose to their level; then, together, they possessed and enjoyed the blessings of Canaan.

Any one or any combination of these reasons may explain why our trials linger even after we receive the Word willingly into our boats.

∼

The apostles' troubled night passage of Galilee (John 6:15–21) is not recorded to illustrate trials that end at appointed times. Rather it portrays those that linger unduly because, like Jonah, we stubbornly refuse to let God have His way.

Despite his extremely perilous and painful circumstances, Jonah sat silently in the fish's belly, resisting the inevitable. His knowledge of God made him sure of one thing: He would have to confess his sins to be released. Yet, stubbornly, he refused to act on this knowledge quickly. Three long, torturous days passed while the disgruntled prophet refused to receive Jesus into his "boat." (See Jonah 1:17; 2:1.) Then suddenly, the spiritual standoff ended. Jonah confessed his rebellion, gave a sacrifice of praise and voiced his willingness to go to Nineveh (v. 9). That very moment he escaped! "The LORD spoke unto the fish, and it vomited out Jonah upon the dry land" (v. 10). At once he reached the shore he longed for. Jonah then discovered the truth the apostles found centuries later…that the moment of human willingness is the moment of divine assistance.

Why not rediscover this truth in your own trials? One thing is certain: An unwilling heart has never yet walked on water—and never will. Nor can it endure the many afflictions God permits to further our spiritual growth.

Chapter Eight

MORE AFFLICTION BRINGS MORE GROWTH

But the more they afflicted them, the more they multiplied and grew.

—EXODUS 1:12

Fearing that the rapidly increasing Israelites would soon threaten his own people, Pharaoh devised a malicious plan to stop their growth. (See Exodus 1:1–14.) He would subject them to the bitterest kind of slavery, giving them incredible workloads and setting over them cruel taskmasters to brutalize them daily. This bitter affliction, he was sure, would weaken them and reduce their numbers. As a result, Egypt and his throne would be secure.

But to Pharaoh's dismay the execution of his plan produced just the opposite: The strength and numbers of the chosen people *increased*. Triumphantly the Scripture notes:

> But the more they afflicted them, the more they multi-
> plied and grew.
>
> —Exodus 1:12

How shocked and frustrated Pharaoh must have been! His intention was to afflict, to "distress with mental or bodily pain; to trouble greatly or grievously." Yet his curse had only blessed the chosen people! Israel's growth in the midst of her affliction was no accident, no stroke of chance or luck. It was the Lord's doing—and it is marvelous in our eyes. The same miracle occurred centuries later on a different stage and with different players.

When the fledgling church began to grow in number and in influence in Jerusalem, the apostate Jewish leaders, alarmed, decided something had to be done to stop what was fast becoming a formidable threat to their religion. So, like Pharaoh, they too devised an evil plan. They would do their worst to the people of the Way and snuff them out. But to their chagrin, the more they afflicted Jesus' followers, the more they multiplied and grew. Both the scope of the gospel and the number of Christians steadily increased. The Book of Acts chronicles the amazing story.

The initial Jewish persecution came in steadily increasing waves. First, Peter and John were arrested for preaching the resurrection of Christ in the temple courts, jailed and warned sternly by the highest court in the land "not to speak at all nor teach in the name of Jesus" (Acts 4:18; see verses 1–22). But they bravely continued preaching the Word in the power of the Spirit (vv. 23–33). Soon the apostles were again arrested for their work and jailed; this time they were beaten (Acts 5:17–40). But again they bravely continued teaching the Word in the power of the Spirit (vv. 41–42). Shaken by their failure to stop Jesus' followers, the Jews then took drastic measures. They arrested the extraordinary deacon Stephen, falsely convicted him of blasphemy, and summarily and illegally executed him. (See Acts 6:9–7:60.) This crime let loose the floodgates of religious hatred in Jerusalem, and soon there arose the most imposing wave of persecution to date—a spiritual tsunami that threatened to drown the entire church in oblivion: "At that time there was a great persecution against the church which was at Jerusalem," and as a result, the saints "were all scattered abroad throughout the regions of Judea and Samaria" (Acts 8:1). The church's situation then looked very bad. To all Jerusalem it seemed clear that the once-glorious *ecclesia* had reached an abrupt and inglorious end. But it had not.

The ultimate, all-powerful strategist, God merely used the Jewish expulsion as His means of propulsion. His invisible, ruling hand was back of the raging Jewish persecutors, benevolently propelling His people toward their predestined places of service and fruitfulness. The heavenly Farmer was sending forth His laborers to plant the seeds of eternal life: "Therefore, they that were scattered abroad went everywhere preaching the word" (v. 4). And just where did He send His sower-witnesses? Precisely where Jesus said they would go.

At His ascension, Jesus prophesied the predestined course of the gospel and its messengers: "Ye shall be witnesses unto me both in Jerusalem, and in all Judea, and in Samaria, and unto the uttermost part of the earth" (Acts 1:8). Consequently, Jerusalem's persecuted believers were driven to the very places Jesus had cited. First, they visited the local districts: "They were all scattered abroad throughout the regions of Judea" (Acts 8:1). Second, they ventured into Samaria: "and Samaria" (v. 1). Philip's evangelistic exploits there are documented in the verses that follow. (See Acts 8:5–25.) Third, the Spirit led them in a bi-directional thrust to reach "the uttermost part of the earth" (Acts 1:8). Southward, the vast continent of Africa was reached through Philip's evangelism of the homeward-bound Ethiopian eunuch who, according to tradition, took Christianity to his native land. (See Acts 8:26–39.) Northward, the regions of Syria, Asia Minor and Macedonia (the European continent) were reached through the founding of the church in Antioch, which became the base for Paul's apostolic missions to these distant fields. (See Acts 11:19–26.) Thus began the fulfillment of Christ's prophecy for the evangelization of the world in this church age, and we see that what looked like an uncontrolled flight caused by malicious enemies was in fact a divinely controlled program of church growth. So the church overcame its initial external persecution.

Meanwhile, Satan also afflicted the church from within. Prejudice raised its ugly head and threatened to divide the saints. Just when "the number of the disciples was multiplied" (Acts 6:1), it became known that the Hellenist Christian widows were not receiving their fair share of food because favoritism was being shown to their Hebrew counterparts. The enemy inspired this injustice, hoping that its exposé would pit the Hellenist Christians against their Hebrew brethren. Then, divided and at strife, the saints would lose their spiritual power. Soon they would decrease in number, the revival would cease, and the people of Jerusalem would be left in the deadly grip of apostate Judaism. It was the enemy's oldest ploy—divide and conquer.

But again, the opposite ensued. The Spirit of God transformed a hindrance into a help. First, He enabled the apostles to quickly and graciously correct the food distribution problem, averting a deadly schism. Second, He used the incident to show them they needed able men to handle the congregation's growing administrative needs. This led to the establishment of the deaconry and the prayerful appointment and ordination of the first deacons. (See Acts 6:2–6.) After these changes were made, God blessed the church with remarkable growth: "And the word of God increased, and the number of the disciples multiplied in Jerusalem greatly" (v. 7). Satan's devious plan was totally reversed: Instead of losing disciples, the church *gained* a large number of new believers—even priests—from the Jewish community: "And a great company of the [Jewish] priests were [converted and became] obedient to the [Christian] faith" (v. 7). So the church also overcame its initial internal opposition.

We see here the same distinctive pattern seen originally in Pharaoh's persecution of Israel in Egypt: Instead of weakening God's people, affliction made them stronger. Instead of decreasing, they increased in every way—numerically, geographically (territorially), organizationally and spiritually.

NUMERICALLY

After each new wave of persecution, the church caught thousands of new fish in its gospel net: "And believers were the more added to the Lord, multitudes both of men and women" (Acts 5:14; see Acts 6:7; 8:5–6; 9:31; 11:19–21). The Jews relived Pharaoh's frustration, as everything they did to lessen the number of believers only increased it. By the thousands Judeans, Syrians, Galatians, Asians, Greeks and Romans were added to the Lord—thanks to the scattering caused by the Jews.

GEOGRAPHICALLY

Before its persecutions began, the church's activities were largely confined to the city of Jerusalem. But with every new lash of distress, its borders were enlarged. More and more, the Light shined into previously unenlightened sectors of the Mediterranean world. Syria, Galatia, Asia Minor, Macedonia, Achaia and finally Italy—one by one these territories received Christ as Lord. And large areas of the world map previously marked for idolatry or atheism were now redrawn as "Christian."

ORGANIZATIONALLY

As the organism of the church grows, so must its organization also; every spurt of new growth requires a certain amount of reorganization. The church's problems with the care of its widows forced the apostles to recognize this and delegate their expanding administrative duties to others.

When the deacons took over the church's business matters and the apostles concentrated solely on its essential spiritual work—the ministry of the Word and prayer (Acts 6:4)—the result was better organization. This paved the way for more numerical and spiritual growth. Because everyone knew their duties and executed them faithfully, large numbers of converts were taken in easily without causing confusion in the ranks. So the organism of the church, the living body of Christ, thrived.

SPIRITUALLY

Hot sunshine hastens the growth of a well-watered, healthy plant. And, uncomfortable as it was, the heat of affliction nevertheless hastened the spiritual growth of the first Christians. The vicious Jewish persecutions unintentionally helped those who suffered them by forcing them to mature more rapidly than Christians who were not so tried. And their spiritual growth was in direct proportion to the number of difficulties they overcame; the more unjust afflictions they endured, the more they grew in the faith and grace of Jesus. The result was a rich harvest of spiritual maturity.

Their souls became deeply rooted in the ways of God as they grew accustomed to difficulty and learned to stand fast amid great pressure. The constant threat of a Jewish attack drove Christ's branches to seek strength and inspiration daily from Him, their inexhaustible heavenly Vine; therefore, they formed the habit of walking closely with Him. They were constrained to learn their enemies' tactics, watch for them and counter them; hence their spiritual discernment grew sharp. As they endured hardness, standing firm under bitter attacks, the Spirit gradually conformed these original Christian soldiers into the image of Christ. And as He was, so were they in this world—spiritually minded, loving, fully committed to the heavenly Father's will and bold. Even their enemies recognized their remarkable spiritual growth: "Now when they [the Jewish council] saw the boldness of Peter and John, and perceived that they were unlearned and ignorant men, they marveled; and they took knowledge of them, that they had been with Jesus" (Acts 4:13).

The principle of Exodus 1:12—that more affliction equals more growth—is the spiritual heritage of every true Christian because, as children of faith, we are the spiritual descendants of Abraham: "They who are of faith, the same are the |sons| of Abraham" (Gal. 3:7). But as with any inheritance, our enrichment is not automatic. We must step forward and claim what is ours. That will take faith and submission to the ways of God.

For if we remain true to Jesus Christ, He will certainly permit afflictions to come our way. The disciple is not above his teacher, nor the servant above his lord. If this world has afflicted Jesus, it will—it must!—also afflict us. Besides, it is the express will of God to test us. He must know: Will we trust Him when the chips are down? Will we yield our desires when they clash with His desires? Our tests reveal our true answers to these questions and determine the success or failure of our discipleship. If we refuse to endure our trials, we will never be Christ's servants. But if we submit to His desire to test us, abide in Him and obey His Word amid our difficulties, we will—we must!—ultimately bear Him much fruit. Why? Because by such trust and submission we lay claim to our spiritual heritage in Exodus 1:12. Hence, God will—He must!—do for us exactly what He did for Israel in Egypt and the church in Jerusalem. The more our enemies trouble us, the more He will bless us. We will grow in every way—spiritually, numerically, organizationally and geographically.

Personally, your growth will occur in whatever area you have been afflicted. If your financial burdens have been increased, God will increase you financially so that your income always exceeds your expenses. If your family has been afflicted, the trouble will ultimately make your family members stronger, wiser and more loving. If your church has been attacked, spiritual, numerical and organizational growth will result in due season. If your ministry has been afflicted, a larger, more effective outreach will emerge from the ashes of your trial. And more importantly, whatever your kind of trial, your faith in God, your heavenly Father, will grow. And that will make you rich!

Something wondrously valuable—unshakable, permanent confidence in an unchanging, unfailing Father-God—is born within your soul when you walk trustingly with God through a long, dark valley of affliction and at last see Him open a way of escape you never thought possible. On the far side of such afflictions you inherit an eternal spiritual fortune, "gold tried in the fire" (Rev. 3:18), a positivism so strong that it dispels all fears of potential future afflictions. You will never be intimidated again because you will know, with childlike simplicity, that what God has done for you before He will do again. David received this indomitable faith when, after enduring a long night-season of weeping, he emerged into a joyful day of blessing. To encourage us, he wrote, "Weeping may endure for a night, but joy cometh in the morning. And in my [newfound, godly] prosperity [given me on the far side of my affliction] I said, *I shall never be moved*" (Ps. 30:5–6, emphasis added).

So, my friend, believe David's advice. Endure your night of affliction *knowing* that it will—it must!—be followed by a day of joyful increases. Whenever the enemy afflicts you, don't focus on your affliction. That will move you from trust in God. Instead, lift up your eyes and focus on all the growth that will be yours at trial's end. That is the rich spiritual inheritance God has willed to you in Exodus 1:12; step forward and claim it by faith and patience. Occupy till it comes. Wait for it. Believe for it. Expect it. Anticipate it. Praise God for it. It will come, yes, it will come—for the enemy can't hold you down.

Chapter Nine

You Can't Keep a God-Man Down!

And the patriarchs...sold Joseph into Egypt; but God was with him, and delivered him out of all his afflictions.

—Acts 7:9–10

The world says you can't keep a good man down. And the biographies of some of its most indomitable sons certainly confirm this—Abraham Lincoln, Theodore Roosevelt, Sir Winston Churchill and, more recently, Nelson Mandela, to name a few. These passed through long, dark valleys of adversity, yet they emerged to achieve enduring success. Life put them down, but they refused to stay down.

The Bible teaches its own version of this familiar adage. It reads: You can't keep a God-man down. That is, you can *put* a man (or woman) of God down, but you can't *keep* him (or her) down. Every time you curse him, God will bless him. Every time you block his path, God will take him another way. Every time you exclude him, God will have others take him in. Every time you defeat him, God will raise him to victory. The life of Joseph demonstrates this very clearly.

Joseph's early years were exceptionally secure. As Jacob's favorite son he was doted on, shielded and blessed. But this initial season of favor was short-lived. When he was only seventeen years old, everything suddenly changed. Without warning Joseph was thrust into a pitiless and relentless forge of adversity—the workshop in which divine instruments are made.

There the tenderfooted son of Rachel was not spared. The mettle of his developing character was repeatedly heated and bent until it assumed its predestined and noble form. Genesis 37, 39 and 40 record Joseph's fiery trials. In chapter 37, he was sold into slavery—by his own brothers! In chapter 39, he was wrongfully accused, convicted and imprisoned— because he would *not* sin! And in chapter 40, when he should have been released on appeal, he was forced to languish in prison for two more long years—because someone who owed him a great debt forgot to help him!

During these painful years Joseph redefined resilience, taking it to new heights of glory. Twice he fell into seemingly bottomless death-pits—slavery and prison—yet, by God's grace, he arose and lived again. Twice the agents of the evil one—his brothers and Potiphar's wife—overwhelmingly defeated him, yet he rebounded and in the end won a victory so great that no other mortal has equaled it. Twice every eyewitness swore he was finished, yet God raised him from a bitter end to a sweet new beginning.

When Joseph's brothers watched him walk away behind his new Midianite master, chained as common chattel, they surely thought they were beholding their brother for the last time. The dreamer and his dreams were *finis*. Ten years later Potiphar's servants surely held the same opinion when, stunned, they saw Joseph, their highly successful and youthful boss, chained and led off to the royal dungeon—the very prison he had superintended as Potiphar's chief steward. (Compare Genesis 40:3; 41:10, 12.) His future then seemed a foregone and dismal conclusion. Never again would he be free. Never again would his works prosper. Never again would his father's God shine upon him with favor.

But on both occasions Joseph's somber observers were wrong. Why? They had overlooked the greatest of all facts— the living God. Twice He intervened in Joseph's troubled life to create a strange yet undeniable spectacle—the prosperity of a ruined man.

RUINED IN SLAVERY

As Joseph shuffled along in leg irons toward Egypt, it must have hit him: His life was ruined. He was a slave now, with little chance for freedom, advancement or a return to Canaan. But then God entered the picture. And miraculously, as Potiphar's slave, Joseph began to prosper: "And the LORD was with Joseph, and he was a prosperous man" (Gen. 39:2). In short order he became a living paradox—a successful failure.

Positionally, everything was adverse for Joseph in Potiphar's house. He was out of place, in Egypt, when he should have been in Canaan. He was in the wrong social class, a slave, though he had been born free. And he was a victim of injustice, being persecuted by brothers to whom he had done only good. Personally, however, everything was prosperous for Joseph. He enjoyed God's comforting and energizing presence: "But God was with him" (Acts 7:9). And this inner blessing overflowed into his daily labors. God prospered his work remarkably: "The LORD made all that he did to prosper in his hand" (Gen. 39:3). He also gave Joseph favor, causing Potiphar to notice his young servant's industriousness: "And his master saw that the LORD was with him…and Joseph found grace in his sight" (vv. 3–4). Realizing he had found a good man, Potiphar promoted Joseph to chief steward: "And he made him overseer over his house, and all that he had he put into his hand" (v. 4). Joseph's personal blessing then overflowed to everyone around him. God caused Potiphar's entire household to thrive: "And it came to pass...the LORD blessed the Egyptian's house for Joseph's sake; and the blessing of the LORD was upon all that he had in the house, and in the field" (v. 5). Everything was different now. Though Joseph had been cast down, he was down no more.

For as Potiphar's steward, Joseph held the most important position in one of Egypt's most important households. As captain of Pharaoh's personal guards, chief executioner and keeper of the royal dungeon, Potiphar was no obscure fellow. He was a courtier of the mighty pharaoh of Egypt—arguably the most powerful man in the world—and hence a member of his select circle of trusted friends and advisors. A comparable person today would be a member of the cabinet of the president of the United States of America. Joseph's stewardship over Potiphar's estate, therefore, was a very public exhibition that every Egyptian beheld, yet none could explain: A Hebrew slave-boy who entered Egypt wearing nothing but a thin shroud of failure now stood before them clothed in beautiful robes of success. Outwardly Joseph's star had fallen, for he was still a slave. But inwardly it was rising. And fast.

RUINED IN PRISON

But as it streaked scintillatingly through the Egyptian sky, Joseph's up-and-coming career suddenly took a sharp downward turn, as the ruin from which he had previously escaped overtook him again with a vengeance. If asked to name a day worse than the one in which his own brothers sold him into slavery, Joseph would have been hard pressed to give an answer...that is, until the day Potiphar's wife vented her wrath upon him. (See Genesis 39:7–20.) That was the blackest day in his darkest years. When Joseph, convicted of a crime he refused to commit, quietly entered his cell in Potiphar's prison, all his blossoming hopes wilted and all his former fears of failure reappeared to haunt the margins of his mind.

But again, God intervened to rebuild the ruins of Joseph's life. Despite Joseph's external adversity, he soon began prospering internally. It was déjà vu—the pattern of advancement seen in his slavery period repeated itself in his prison experience. With divine precision, each step of his earlier success was duplicated.

He now served the jailer diligently, just as he had Potiphar. (See Genesis 39:20–23, 3–4.) And God prospered everything Joseph did for the jailer, just as He had blessed all his works for Potiphar: "The LORD was with him, and that which he did, the LORD made it to prosper" (v. 23; see verses 2–3). God also gave him favor with the jailer, just as He had done with Potiphar: "But the LORD...gave him favor in the sight of the keeper of the prison" (v. 21; see verse 4). The jailer then promoted Joseph to prison administrator, just as Potiphar had raised him to chief steward: "And the keeper of the prison committed to Joseph's hand all the prisoners that were in the prison" (v. 22; see verse 4). The jailer also put complete trust in Joseph, just as Potiphar had: "The keeper of the prison looked not to anything that was under his hand; because the LORD was with him [Joseph]" (v. 23; see verse 6). God then caused the entire prison to prosper, exactly as Potiphar's estate had thrived while under Joseph's supervision. (See verse 5.) Several facts reveal this. The prisoners were blessed by Joseph's faithful and efficient service: "Whatsoever they did there, he [Joseph] was the doer of it" (v. 22). "And he [Joseph] served them" (Gen. 40:4). The prison's gloomy atmosphere was lightened by Joseph's cheerful attitude. (See Genesis 40:6–7.) By freely exercising his gift of interpretation, Joseph ministered to the prisoners, especially

Pharaoh's butler: "And Joseph said unto him, This is the interpretation of it" (v. 12; see verses 8–19; 41:12–13).

All this extraordinary spiritual prosperity occurred in a season of extraordinary adversity. Though from every worldly perspective Joseph was still a ruined man, his spiritual life and ministry gift were flourishing. Though cast down, he was not downcast. And soon he would rise above his ruin a final time. And fast. In fact, Joseph's was the fastest rising star in Egypt.

Raised in Power

In the hour it is needed, "a man's gift maketh room for him, and bringeth him before great men" (Prov. 18:16). So the proverb asserts, and so it was with Joseph. When God chose to reveal the coming famine to Pharaoh through a dream, only Joseph had the gift Pharaoh needed. (See Genesis 41:1–52.) When Pharaoh asked his magicians and wise men for an interpretation, all their omens, incantations and occult methodology failed. Try as they might, they simply could not interpret Pharaoh's dream. And why? God had reserved that honor, and the approaching hour, for Joseph. Finally, the time had come for his gift to make room for him.

So at the butler's belated suggestion, Joseph was called in before the king. (See Genesis 41:9–14.) What unfolded then was another great paradox: For several hours a lowly Hebrew slave, who had been despised, convicted and forgotten, commanded the undivided attention of the lofty ruler of the Nile, who sat spellbound as Joseph delivered his divinely inspired interpretation and plan. And the miracle didn't stop there. Pharaoh actually *believed* Joseph and immediately implemented his proposed plan of action! Moreover, he made Joseph his prime minister and endowed him with far-reaching authority, regal honor, immense wealth, a palatial home and a noble wife. Joseph's instant establishment at the highest level of Egyptian life defied reasonable explanation. It was simply

God! He wouldn't let the world keep His man down. Here is an inspiring lesson for us all.

~

When we grow in God's Word or blossom in His work, eventually the enemy will in some way try to put us down. With God's permission, he will betray us into a pit of rejection or a prison of hindrance, rendering us temporarily unable to advance. In our apparent ruin we may find ourselves quite discouraged and ready to quit the race set before us. After all, what can a ruined Christian do?

It is then that we must remember Joseph's experiences. Amid defeat, his soul was so filled with the Spirit of victory that the angel of defeat simply couldn't hold him. Every time Satan put him down, God raised him up. Every time Satan ruined him, Joseph rose above the ruin. Not immediately, but steadily and surely. Both as a slave and a prisoner Joseph walked on the turbulent waters of his life by simply occupying patiently and trusting God to help him. Then one day, at God's appointed time, there was a great calm, and Joseph was released from all his buffetings. It can be the same with us.

If in every stormy season of our lives we perseveringly trust and obey God, God will always be with us: "For he hath said, I will *never* leave thee, nor forsake thee" (Heb. 13:5, emphasis added). And when God is with us, even if we're in the most impossible circumstances, we may still overcome our troubled waters; that is, serve Christ and Christianity faithfully, prosper, advance, gain favor and at last rise above our ruinous storm. And why?

Because you can't keep a God-man down! Both his God and he are just too persistent.

Chapter Ten

RIGHT AND WRONG
PERSISTENCE

Yet because of his shameless persistence and insistence,
he will get up and give him as much as he needs.

—LUKE 11:8, AMP

To persist is to continue steadfastly in one's course of action despite delays, opposition or failure. It is to refuse to give up a desired end, to insist—repetitively, obstinately, tenaciously—that one's goal be realized. Persistence is a priceless character trait.

Without exception, great achievers are persistent souls. Since ancient times, people of ordinary skill, strength and wisdom have done extraordinary things merely because they refused to give up. They fixed their mind's eye on a noble goal and pursued it relentlessly, and eventually their effort paid off. If we are to be fruitful servants of Christ, souls who know their God and are strong and do exploits, and if we hope to spend more time walking on water than treading it, one thing is certain: We must be persistent.

In learning to persist, however, we must realize that not all persistence is pleasing to God. There are both right and wrong kinds of persistence. There are times when God wants us to press on and, as Sir Winston Churchill said:

> NEVER GIVE IN. NEVER GIVE IN.
> NEVER, NEVER, NEVER, NEVER . . .

And there are other times when He wants us to do just the opposite—abandon our effort at the earliest opportunity. Our persistence, then, must be guided by discernment. Foolish Christians persist blindly, oblivious to the signs of heaven, but the wise persevere with sensitivity, their hearts ever ready to perceive God's voice. Well do they know that there is a time to persist and a time to relent. The Scriptures describe several persons who persisted wrongly.

AHIMAAZ

In 2 Samuel 18:19–33, Ahimaaz asked permission to carry word to King David that Absalom's rebellion had been quelled. Joab promptly denied his request: "Thou shalt not bear tidings this day, but thou shalt bear tidings another day" (v. 20). And Ahimaaz promptly refused to take no for an answer. Despite Joab's clear denial and the knowledge that another man, the Cushite, had been appointed the king's messenger that day, Ahimaaz persisted, requesting permission to run two more times (vv. 22–23). Exasperated, Joab finally gave him leave: "And he said unto him, Run" (v. 23). So, happy with his "victory," Ahimaaz rushed off to bear tidings to King David.

When he arrived, however, he soon lost his joy. For

immediately after he delivered his untrue and unsatisfactory report, the Cushite arrived and told David the whole story… Absalom was dead. (See 2 Samuel 18:20, 32.) Ahimaaz then looked, and felt, quite foolish—and deservedly so. He had persisted and had gotten his way, but for what? The end of his persistence was sheer futility and humiliation.

THE ISRAELITES

During their wilderness wanderings, the Israelites became discontent with God's provision of manna and began openly lusting for meat: "And the children of Israel also wept again, and said, Who shall give us flesh to eat?" (Num. 11:4; see verses 5–6). Their gross unthankfulness and unchecked lust grieved God's heart. But rather than repent of their selfish desire, the people persisted in it. Again and again they cried in the ears of Moses and God for meat. Finally, God's patience expired and He issued a judgment: He gave them the meat they so stubbornly demanded, but at a dreadfully high price—they were cut off spiritually, deprived of His favor and fellowship: "And he gave them their request, but sent leanness into their soul" (Ps. 106:15; see Numbers 11:33–34). So their persistence led to spiritual dryness.

DELILAH

Motivated by the Philistines' offer of a huge financial reward, Delilah begged Samson three times to reveal the secret of his strength. (See Judges 16:4–21.) But, unwilling to surrender that vital information, Samson responded each time with deceit. Many women, after such decisive failure, would have let the matter drop. But not Delilah. She was tenacity incarnate. Daily she waged psychological warfare on her psychologically weaker victim, insisting and *insisting* and *insisting* that Samson tell her his secret: "She pressed him daily with her words, and urged him" (v. 16). Finally, her insistence overcame his resistance and "he told her all his heart" (v. 17). She then promptly cashed in the information for her reward (v. 18).

Other biblical examples vividly portray godly persistence.

THE SYROPHENICIAN WOMAN

With her daughter in desperate need of deliverance, the Syrophenician woman set herself to seek help from Jesus. (See Matthew 15:21–28.) But hers would be no easy path to victory.

Strangely, her first cry for mercy was met by complete silence. The compassionate One turned away in apparent callousness (v. 23). But the needy mother persisted, next begging help from His disciples who, irritated, asked Jesus to send her away (v. 23). Jesus then disappointed her again by sending word that He was sent to minister to Jews—not Gentiles like herself (v. 24). But still she hung in there. Falling before Him, she begged unashamedly, "Lord, help me" (v. 25). Jesus' response then was shocking: He openly insulted her, referring to her as a Gentile dog: "It is not |right| to take the children's bread, and to cast it to *dogs*" (v. 26, emphasis added). But she was prepared even for this, meeting His third strange denial with her fourth humble request: "Truth, Lord; yet the dogs eat of the crumbs which fall from their master's table" (v. 27). Her extraordinary persistence won an immediate response. Without delay, Jesus gave her both deliverance and praise: "O woman, great is thy faith; be it unto thee even as thou wilt" (v. 28).

THE WIDOW AND THE UNJUST JUDGE

In one of His parables, Jesus described a widow who was denied justice by a callous judge (Luke 18:1–8). Apparently he was content to leave her to the oppression of her adversary. But apparently she wasn't. So she got after him. Every day she came into his court, always with the same cry: "Give me justice against my adversary" (v. 3, AMP). Eventually her amazing steadfastness overcame his amazing indifference, and, to save his own sanity, he agreed to help her, concluding, "Yet because this widow troubleth me, I will avenge her, lest by her continual coming she weary me" (v. 5). *The New Testament in Modern English*, by J.B. Phillips, translates his ruling: "Yet this woman is such a nuisance that I shall give judgment in her favour, or else her continual visits will be the death of me!" So, at long last, she received justice.

DANIEL

Deeply concerned for the future of his people, Daniel felt led to discover and then record what would befall the Jews in the latter days. (See Daniel 10:1–21.) So he set himself to seek the Lord daily, searching the Scriptures (v. 21), fasting (vv. 2–3) and petitioning heaven for understanding (v. 12). But strangely, God's answer was not forthcoming. For days heaven left its prime spokesman in the dark. This nonresponse puzzled Daniel, for his petitions were usually answered promptly. Nevertheless, at some point he made a very simple but wise decision: He would just continue doing what he had been doing until he heard from God. Finally, after twenty-one days, his perseverance paid off. An angel, who had been sent by God the day Daniel began praying, visited him and revealed the divine plan: "Now I am come to make thee understand what shall befall thy people in the latter days" (v. 14).

THE PERSISTENT FRIEND

In another parable, Jesus described a man who called on a friend at midnight, seeking bread for another friend who had unexpectedly turned up on his doorstep hungry (Luke 11:5–10). But his urgent request fell on unconcerned ears. His friend replied, "Trouble me not; the door is now shut, and my children are with me in bed" (v. 7). Undaunted, and with no other options available at that hour, the man simply continued knocking at his unfriendly friend's door. Finally, his importunity roused him, and the man arose and gave him all the bread he needed: "Yet because of his shameless persistence and insistence, he will get up and give him as much as he needs" (v. 8, AMP).

~

THE DIFFERENCE IS *INWARD*

Outwardly, there is no discernable difference between godly and ungodly persistence. The foregoing examples show us that they often look exactly the same. Delilah pressed Samson just as relentlessly as the Syrophenician did Jesus. And Daniel sought wisdom just as fervently as Ahimaaz sought a chance to run. The difference is inward. It lies in the motive, the end that is sought. Godly persistence seeks the will of God—His plan, His calling or something pleasing in His sight. Or it seeks something for the sake of justice or mercy. And it often benefits not just one person but many. Ungodly persistence, however, seeks solely the will of self. It is a narrow-minded effort that is prideful, lustful or covetous in spirit and usually ignores the welfare of others. Again, the examples given above confirm this.

Ahimaaz persisted with Joab because he was proud and longed for the honor of being the king's messenger. He was absolutely unconcerned with the accuracy of his tidings or their effect on David's troubled soul. The Israelites persistently cried to Moses for flesh because they were lustful. Unthankful to God and discontented with His gracious provision of manna, they wanted only to satisfy their fleshly cravings. Delilah pursued a relationship with Samson for only one reason—money. Once she got it, she lost no sleep over the cruel demise of her "true love."

On the other hand, the Syrophenician woman followed hard after Christ solely to help another—her troubled daughter. And while the widow was insistent with the unjust judge in her own cause, the context implies that she was being terribly oppressed by her adversary. Hence her cause was just;

her mistreatment, grievous; and her need of relief, great. Daniel pursued spiritual knowledge because his people desperately needed hope to give them the strength to endure their bitter captivity. Indeed, his revelations lightened multitudes of heavy Jewish hearts. And the persistent friend sought bread to feed his hungry visitor, not himself. All of these righteous "persisters" sought the will of God, justice or mercy. There was nothing sinful or selfish about their efforts. They won deliverance for the tormented, justice for the oppressed, food for the hungry and encouraging truths for God's people. We should each imitate their persistence.

THE CAUSES AND CONCLUSIONS OF SELF-EXAMINATION

After persisting long in a cause without success, doubts and questions naturally arise. We wonder, "Is my persistence right or wrong? Is this the Lord's cause or just a selfish desire of my own? Is the opposition I'm facing demonic or divine—is Satan trying to stop me short of a blessing, or is God trying to tell me I'm on the wrong road?" When these thoughts come, it's time to seek the Lord. We need either confirmation or correction from on high.

For that we must examine ourselves with brutal frankness. What are our true motives? Is the Spirit of truth urging us to give up, yet we still find ourselves selfishly driven to go further? Or would we really *love* to quit but cannot honestly do so without the conviction that we are failing God? These questions must be answered with the most sterile honesty. Such self-examination will result in one of three conclusions:

We are sure our persistence is God's will.

If you are convinced that your effort is God's will, banish doubt and persist. Diligently ignore all subsequent doubts concerning the matter, lest you reopen a case the Spirit of God has closed. And don't fret at the passing of time. God will reward your perseverance in His time, and His time is never too late.

We are sure our persistence is not His will.

If you are sure your cause is not God's will, you should abandon your effort immediately—and permanently. Never again knock on a door when you know Jesus has closed it. First, those doors can't be opened. Jesus is "he that...shutteth, and *no man openeth*" (Rev. 3:7, emphasis added). You will only waste your own time and energy and grieve Him by further persistence. Second, if you refuse to yield to His clearly revealed will, the Lord may chasten you, as He did the Israelites, by permitting you to pry a door open to your own undoing. You may get what you lust for but lose what you live by—the Lord's presence, approval, peace, strength and voice in your life—and that for a long, long time. Make no mistake: We pay a high price for self-willed persistence. There is one exception to this.

Sometimes the Lord permits doors to be shut temporarily; then He opens them at a later time. In such cases, the end we seek is His will, but His time has not yet come. For example, the Holy Spirit expressly forbade Paul to preach in Asia Minor, thus clearly closing that door at that time, because a more timely need existed in Macedonia. (See Acts 16:6–10.) Yet sometime later He led Paul to Asia Minor and greatly blessed his work there. (See Acts 19.) Also, a door may be shut because a satanic hinderer—someone indifferent or opposed to His will, such as a carnal Christian or an enemy of the gospel—is resisting its opening. Again, in the example given above, when the persistent friend first knocked at his sleepy friend's residence, the door was "*now* [or *then*] shut" (Luke 11:7, emphasis added). Later, as he continued knocking, the same door—not a different one—was opened, and he was given all the bread he needed. That this door was at last opened with God's full blessing (implied) proves that he had knocked on the right door from the beginning. Therefore, it hadn't been shut by God, but solely by his friend's ungracious negligence. God permitted this hindrance to give his servant an opportunity to practice the grace of persistence. Remember, persistence cannot be perfected without resistance.

It may be the same with you. If God is truly leading, the door that is "*now* shut" will open for you later, when God's time fully comes or when by prayer and persistence you break through the work of the hinderer. (See Romans 1:13; 1 Thessalonians 2:18.)

We are still unsure.

If you are still unsure of God's will, temporarily stop pursuing the matter and wait on the Lord. Talk openly to Him in prayer, asking Him to show you His will: "And they prayed, and said, Thou, Lord,...show which of these two thou hast chosen" (Acts 1:24). Be honest; tell Him exactly what you want or wish or think about the matter. Express your true heart's desire, not what you think He wants you to say. Then be submissive: Waive your rights and surrender your will to your heavenly Father's will, putting His desires before yours. This is what Jesus did in the garden: "Abba, Father...Take away this cup from me; nevertheless, not what I will, but what thou wilt" (Mark 14:36). Finally, be patient. Go on with your normal affairs, trusting God to speak to you. The Communicator can quicken His Word to your heart in a thousand ways. Be assured, this kind of waiting cannot hurt. If immediate action is needed, God will speak to you immediately. If He doesn't speak immediately, immediate action is not needed. Continue this until He reveals His will.

Once He does so, with confirmation, then act with complete confidence, either resuming or abandoning your persistence as He wills.

Let the Peace of God Rule

Your internal reaction to your new or renewed course of action will further confirm God's will. When you face truth and act on it, your heart is immediately freer. Why? Because of Christ's law of truth: "The truth shall make you free" (John 8:32). All the agitation of anxiety ceases, doubt flees, and deep peace, the peace of God that passes all understanding, fills your heart. Even if outward difficulties persist, your soul will dwell at ease. This is God's quiet, internal witness that you are on the right course: "Her [divine wisdom's] ways are ways of pleasantness, and all her paths are [result in] peace [inward heart-rest]" (Prov. 3:17; see Psalm 25:12–13). But if you disobey the conclusions of your self-examination and lie to yourself (saying "peace, peace" when you don't have peace), you will not have a quiet heart. Instead, your inward confusion and misery will intensify. Why? Because, by the inward pressure of His Spirit, God Himself is resisting you for your proud defiance of His will: "God resisteth the proud" (James 4:6).

So take the advice of the apostle Paul: "And let the peace (soul harmony which comes) from the Christ rule (act as umpire continually) in your hearts—deciding and settling with finality all questions that arise in your minds" (Col. 3:15, AMP). If yours is the right kind of persistence and you stop, your peace will go from you because God wants you to persist. And if your persistence is wrong and you continue, your peace will go from you because God wants you to stop. Whatever the ruling handed down by Judge Peace, obey it. That will keep you on course to fulfill your destiny.

Chapter Eleven

THE LOVE
THAT HURTS

He sent a man before them, even Joseph...whose feet
they hurt with fetters.

—PSALM 105:17–18

Destiny is a very important word to God. In a Christian
context, it means all that God intends us to be and to
do in Christ Jesus, both in this world and the next.

Every true Christian is a predestined soul. The apostle
Paul reveals, "For whom he did foreknow, he also did *predestinate*...moreover, whom he did *predestinate*, them he also called"
(Rom. 8:29–30, emphasis added). Simply put, the marvel of
predestination is based upon God's marvelous foreknowledge:
"For whom he did *foreknow*..." (emphasis added). In His marvelous foreknowledge, God knows exactly how every personal-
ity will develop. Sure of our response to the gospel message,
the authority of His Word, the instruction of our teachers, the

correction of our counselors, the chastening of the Holy Spirit and the blessings and adversities of life, He fashions for every Christian a spiritual destiny—a personal identity and a particular work that fulfills a part of His universal plan for His people. And He does this before we are born. In fact, He did it before the world was created: "According as he hath chosen us in him before the foundation of the world…having predestinated us" (Eph.1:4–5; see 2:10). Hence, our destinies as Christians are fully predetermined by God. (Unbelievers are also predestined, but to an inglorious work and end, as we see in Romans 9:17–18, 22.) Because predestation exceeds the limits of our finite minds, it is a mystery. But because the Bible asserts it, it is a fact in which we should strongly believe.

EXAMPLES OF PREDESTINATION: THUS SAITH THE SCRIPTURE

Evidence of predestination abounds in Scripture. Consider these lucid examples of divine foreknowledge and predetermination of service.

The apostle Paul

The apostle Paul was destined primarily to preach to the Gentiles and testify before kings. Of him the Predestinator said, "He is a chosen vessel unto me, to bear my name before the Gentiles, and kings" (Acts 9:15). Paul was also called to suffer every sort of tribulation and persecution imaginable, that the record of his adverse experiences might become a "pattern" of Christian suffering for all time. Paul himself testified, "For this cause I obtained mercy, that in me first Jesus Christ might show forth all long-suffering, *for a pattern* to them who should hereafter believe on him" (1 Tim. 1:16, emphasis added; see Acts 9:16).

Samson

Before Samson's conception, his destiny was capsulated in the inspired words of the angel of the Lord: "And he shall begin to deliver Israel out of the hand of the Philistines" (Judg. 13:5).

Jeremiah

Jeremiah's destiny also was settled long before his conception. The Lord informed him, "Before I formed thee in the |womb|, I knew thee; and before thou camest forth out of the womb, I sanctified thee, and I ordained thee a prophet unto the nations" (Jer. 1:5).

John the Baptist

The destiny of John the Baptist—Israel's dynamic reformer and Messiah's personal forerunner—was announced by the angel Gabriel before his conception: "For he shall be great in the sight of the Lord…and many of the children of Israel shall he turn to the Lord, their God. And he shall go before him in the spirit and power of Elijah…to make ready a people prepared for the Lord" (Luke 1:15–17). Seven centuries earlier, the same had been foreseen and written by the prophet Isaiah (Isa. 40:3–5).

Esther

Esther was destined to be an instrument of deliverance for her people at one of the most crucial points in their history. With inspiration Mordecai pointed out to her, "Who knoweth whether thou art come to the kingdom *for such a time as this?*" (Esther 4:14, emphasis added).

The apostle Peter

Though a fishermen by trade, Simon, the son of Jonah, was destined to become Peter, the apostle, and "catch" many men for Jesus. So Jesus informed him, "Henceforth thou shalt catch men" (Luke 5:10; see Acts 2:41).

∼

Has it ever hit us? We too have been predestinated by God. As we grow in knowing God and walking closely with

Him, fulfilling our spiritual destiny becomes ever more important to us. Increasingly we realize that when we stand before the judgment seat of Christ, that alone will matter. At that moment, worldly achievements, wealth and popularity—things still cherished by most believers in this Laodicean age—will mean nothing. Has it sunk in on us that every deed done in "the lust of the flesh," "the lust of the eyes" and, most notably, for "the pride of life" (see 1 John 2:15–17) is worth *nothing?!* The only thing Judge Jesus will ask is: Did we become all He created us to be and do all He created us to do? This issue of destiny captivated the apostle Paul. Daily he grew ever more determined to fulfill the purpose of his creation and salvation: "I follow after, if that I may apprehend that for which also I am apprehended of Christ Jesus" (Phil. 3:12). What about us? Are we "following after" the path of our spiritual destiny?

Led by a Higher Love and Reason

God leads us down the path of destiny with a love and reason infinitely higher than our own. Through the prophet Isaiah He declared:

> For my thoughts are not your thoughts, neither are your ways my ways, saith the Lord. For as the heavens are higher than the earth, so are my ways higher than your ways, and my thoughts than your thoughts.
>
> —Isaiah 55:8–9

Human love typically refuses to allow its loved ones to suffer, even if such is necessary to obtain a desirable end. But God's love reasons differently. *He sometimes permits us to be hurt to drive us into the place of fruitfulness and destiny.* Why? Because He takes the long view of our lives. Always He sees the present in full view of the future and time as merely the prelude to eternity. He reasons that the prize of everlasting joy is well worth the price of temporary pain. Hence, He is willing to let us suffer, if such suffering may bring us to a "latter end" filled with abundant fruit, overflowing joy and unending glory. Simply put, He who spared not His only Son but sent Him to the cross to fulfill His predestined mission, how shall He spare us our crosses; that is, if we are to fulfill our predestined missions?

JOSEPH: A MAN HURT BY LOVE

Joseph's destiny was fulfilled in Egypt. There God made him amazingly fruitful, as the Spirit of prophecy later noted: "Joseph is a fruitful bough, even a fruitful bough by a well" (Gen. 49:22). But to get to Egypt, Joseph had to suffer. His path of destiny consisted of a series of adversities, not a string of blessings. Brotherly hatred, betrayal, confinement in an empty pit, slavery in a foreign land, sexual temptation, false accusation, prison life, the appearance of being abandoned by God and the fact of being forgotten by men—all these cruel things hurt the favored son of Jacob just as much as the rough iron fetters that chafed and scarred his ankles in Potiphar's dungeon: "He sent a man before them, even Joseph...whose feet they *hurt* with fetters" (Ps. 105:17–18, emphasis added). And here is the point we must heed: Scripture unmistakably asserts that God, not Satan, sent Joseph down this strange highway: "*He [God] sent* a man before them, even Joseph" (emphasis added). And "God," we know, "is love" (1 John 4:16).

That our God, the gracious One, the source and perfection of compassion, ordered such a distressful course for His chosen one is remarkable. Surely, He drew back at the thought of having to hurt Joseph. Joseph was young manhood at its best—trusting, meek, spiritual, upright, loyal, industrious and true. Yet God knew that Joseph's destiny, his fruitfulness in God, was far more important than his immediate personal comfort. So, overruling the objections of His mercy, the all-

105

wise Predestinator gave Satan permission to trouble the waters of Joseph's life. Though not written, it is clear that God said of Joseph, as he did of Job, "Behold, he is in thine hand" (Job 2:6). And for a long season Joseph's whole being—spirit, soul, mind and body—shared the same experience. Unitedly, they hurt.

Not his lengthy bitter trial, but Joseph's *reaction* to it, sealed his appointment with destiny. Because he practiced the attitude of acceptance, choosing to see God in everything that touched his life (see chapter 2), his soul prospered. By faith he acknowledged the Lord in all his ways, gave thanks in every situation and counted it all joy, believing that God would cause every single occurrence—even injustices and delays—to ultimately work together for his good. Consequently, instead of sliding backwards, he marched forward. Instead of degenerating, he generated new spiritual power. Instead of being infected by the gloom of his prison environment, he became infused with the strength of its elements. Nightly, "he was laid in iron" (Ps. 105:18), and, indeed, the iron that bound him entered into his very soul; thus Jacob's softest son was transformed into God's iron man. Furthermore, his spiritual gift (the interpretation of dreams) prospered. He foretold precisely what would befall the butler and baker of Egypt. (See Genesis 40:5–22.) But most importantly, Joseph's misfortunes pressed him nearer to his glorious end. For him, all roads led to "a place where the king's prisoners were bound" (Gen. 39:20)—the very place from which Pharaoh would later call him forth to interpret his dreams, guide Egypt, feed the nations and save the chosen people. During these years Joseph's conviction that God's loving hand was behind every hurt grew so strong that he later asserted it to his brethren *three times* in the same conversation: "God did send me before you to preserve life...God sent me before you to preserve you a posterity...it was not you that sent me here, but God" (Gen. 45:5–8).

PAIN—NECESSARY TO FRUITFULNESS AND DESTINY

All around us we see abundant testimony to this life-fact: Pain is a necessary part of fruitfulness and destiny. Consider the earth's manifold witness.

Destined to nourish us, "bread |grain| is |ground|" (Isa. 28:28). The beautiful kernels are ground beneath pitiless millstones so that meal and, from that, bread may be made. Created to produce wine, grapes are trampled and split in the winepress; only then do their precious juices flow out. Designed to give fragrance, rose petals are plucked off and crushed; then their oil is extracted to make perfume. Made to provide sweetness, maple trees are pierced with holes yearly; then, from their wounds, flow their "fruit," their unusually sweet sap, from which both syrup and sugar are made. Bruising, grinding, splitting, crushing and piercing—these words describe the infliction of pain upon plants—the pain by which they produce their fruit. But such hurts do not make them beautiful.

Undeniably, in the world of plants, fruitfulness and beauty rarely exist together. Good fruit is most often found on trees that are not very picturesque. The reason for this is simple: Fruit trees are marred by the scars of many purgings. Often hurt by the husbandman, they are usually knobby, short and unattractive. Their beauty is not that of an impressive exterior, perfectly symmetrical and upright, but that of a rich, productive interior. Their glory and their destiny lie solely in their fruit.

THE PAINS OF FRUITFUL CHRISTIANS

As in nature, so it is in Christianity. Carnal Christians—those who refuse to seek God's face, obey His Word, respond to His correction or follow His guidance—remain barren and useless to heaven, despite often attaining and preserving an outwardly beautiful life in this present world. But spiritual Christians—those who walk consistently in faith and submissive obedience to God—are invariably predestined to bear much fruit in Christ. Therefore, as productive fruit trees, they are regularly purged and chastened by God. Or, in Jesus' words: "Every branch that beareth fruit, *he purgeth it*" (John 15:2, emphasis added). These spiritually fruitful believers are often wounded by the rejection and hatred of men, as was Joseph: "Joseph is a fruitful bough...the archers have |harassed| him, and shot at him, and hated him" (Gen. 49:22–23; see Luke 21:16–17). Hence, their worldly beauty—the attractiveness of a typically prosperous, outwardly undisturbed life—goes from them. Why? Because their natural life is periodically split, pierced and crushed, even unto death, that their spiritual life, purified and strengthened, may again bud and bring forth more fruit. Again, in Jesus' words: "He purgeth it, that it may bring forth *more fruit*" (John 15:2, emphasis added). Our heavenly Husbandman has a wide assortment of cutters, splitters, piercers, grinders and crushers at His disposal.

For instance, we experience failure in our chosen profession and that after a most determined effort to succeed—and disappointment pierces us. We encounter ridicule and mockery because of our stated beliefs and are forced out of churches, fellowships or ministries in which we had hoped to rise to leadership—and rejection wounds us. Our spouses refuse to honor their marriage vows, and one day we are shocked to find ourselves victims of adultery or abandonment and wrongful divorce—and grief splits our hearts. Good friends quietly turn away and separate us from their company, enemies open their mouths and release floods of slander, and soon people who have never laid eyes on us despise us—and injustice crushes us. Relatives misunderstand our actions and refuse our explanations—and sorrow cuts us. Urgently needed assistance is denied, temporarily shutting down our prayer-born works or ministries—and hindrance grinds us to humility. Thus our whole being, as Joseph's, hurts. Even so, there is hope for us, strong hope; for these are the pains of fruitfulness. And they are inflicted by Love.

Can You—Will You— See the Hand of Love?

Truly, the painful trials of obedient Christians are not random happenings or the result of mere human wills at work. They are the hand of our all-controlling God leading us onward in the way He has chosen. In short, they are the Love that hurts.

It was this Love that caused Laban's face to change and become "not toward" Jacob (Gen. 31:2), because God's time had come for Jacob to return to Bethel and become the princely character he was destined to be. It was this Love that permitted the Jews to raise "great persecution" (Acts 8:1) against the church, because God's time had come to send the gospel on its predestined course to "Samaria, and unto the uttermost part of the earth" (Acts 1:8; see chapter 8, pages 74–76). It was this Love that stirred the Philistine lords to reject David's proffered and skilled military services in their battle with Israel at Mount Gilboa so that David would return to Ziklag, from whence he would soon be called to his predestined throne at Hebron, and so no one could rightfully accuse David of killing his worst enemy, King Saul, who fell in the battle. (See 1 Samuel 29:1–11; 31:1–6.) We see Love's hand so clearly in these passages, yet this doesn't help us at all in our day of trouble. We must see it in our own lives.

For that, we must have faith, for when faith believes, faith sees. The eyes of our understanding detect invisible spiritual realities. Faith enabled Moses to discern the hand of Love at work in his years of pain: "By faith…he endured, as seeing him who is invisible" (Heb. 11:27). But what about you, friend? Can you—will you—see the hand of Love in your hurts?

Has some cruel offense suddenly ripped open your soul, crushed your hopes and threatened your very will to live? Don't let its unfairness move you to rebel; hold fast your confidence in Love. Like Moses, endure as seeing His invisible hand behind your visible perplexities. Then exercise your "believer." Believe that your unfortunate turn of events is God's hand turning you in another direction. Believe that He is spoiling your preferred way to establish you in His predestined way. Believe that He is denying you the good to give you the best. Believe that He is taking you low to later raise you higher than you've ever imagined. And, believing, humbly and wisely yield your will wholly to His. Completely release the course that you have chosen and fully embrace the course that He has chosen for you: "Him shall he teach in the way that *he* shall choose" (Ps. 25:12, emphasis added). Then, like Peter, walk on the raging billows of your affliction. And be upbeat. Love has led countless others to their predestined places of fruitfulness. Why can't He also lead you to yours? So trust Him. And by faith, give Him thanks.

In his classic devotional *My Utmost for His Highest*, Oswald Chambers said bluntly:

> If through a broken heart God can bring His purposes to pass in the world, then thank Him for breaking your heart.

This is a large and incredibly curative pill for Christians who are sick with the pain of fruitfulness. May God give us the understanding and humility to swallow it.

Chapter Twelve

THE TEMPERER

The LORD... he bringeth low, and lifteth up.

—1 SAMUEL 2:7

W hile Love's deep hurts are mercifully few, His temperings are many. It is necessary, then, for every believer to understand the process of spiritual tempering.

Spiritual tempering parallels natural tempering. In this world, tempering is a process by which construction materials are hardened by exposing them alternately to hot and cold conditions. Steel and glass are two substances frequently tempered. After their original manufacture, they are each reheated and then suddenly cooled. This hardens them, making them stronger and more durable. As a result, they are much less likely to fail or break when in use. Natural tempering, therefore, prepares materials to fulfill their intended functions in buildings, homes, bridges and other structures. God also tempers His building materials.

Those materials are His redeemed children, Christians such as you and me. The vast congregation of believers worldwide is the human "stockpile" from which the Spirit is building the End-Time church of Jesus Christ. Upon its soon-coming formation, He will refill it with His glory, just as He did when Israel's tabernacle and temple were erected. The writings of the apostle Paul confirm that Christians are indeed God's building materials. He taught:

> Ye [Christians collectively] are God's building.
>
> —1 CORINTHIANS 3:9

> Know ye not that ye [Christians collectively] are the temple of God, and that the Spirit of God dwelleth in you?
>
> —1 CORINTHIANS 3:16

> In whom ye [Christians collectively] also are built together for an habitation of God through the Spirit.
>
> —EPHESIANS 2:22

In His spiritual tempering process, the Lord deliberately exposes Christians alternately to pleasant (uplifting) and unpleasant (humbling) experiences. Acknowledging Him as both the humbler and exalter of all flesh, and hence of His own people also, Hannah prophesied, "The LORD...he bringeth low [humbles], and lifteth up [exalts]" (1 Sam. 2:7). A remarkable example of this is found in the first part of the Book of Joshua (chapters 3–10). There we find this undeniable evidence of divine tempering:

Chapters 3–4	Uplifting miracle	The Jordan crossing
Chapter 5	Humbling correction	Gilgal—cutting away of the flesh
Chapter 6	Uplifting victory	Jericho

Chapter	7	Humbling defeat	First Battle of Ai; also Achan's judgment
Chapter	8	Uplifting victory	Second Battle of Ai
Chapter	9	Humbling failure	Beguiled by the Gibeonites
Chapter	10	Uplifting victory	Battle of Gibeon

The Lord used this discipline to make Joshua's generation spiritually strong and fit to take the land of Canaan and rule it in the fear of God. And He tempers us today to strengthen our characters so that we may become stable, and hence reliable parts of His mystical ecclesiastical temple. Jesus was, and still is, the Master Temperer of saints.

In the days of His flesh, Jesus constantly guarded His apostles' emotional highs and lows, ever aware of the spiritual dangers that attend periods of excitement and periods of depression. By exposing them to both joy and sorrow periodically, He disciplined, or tempered them, to live life on an even keel. This is most evident in the Gospel of Luke.

THE TEMPERER AT WORK

In Luke 9 and 10, we find a distinct pattern to Christ's actions. When His disciples were too high, He brought them low; when they were too low, He lifted them up. When they overheated, He cooled them off; when they became cold, He warmed them.

Luke 9

In verses 18–21 we read of the apostles being lifted up by a heavenly revelation. One day while Jesus and the Twelve were talking, the Spirit suddenly illuminated Peter with the full awareness of Jesus' deity. Thrilled, Peter immediately shared the light: "Peter, answering, said, [Thou art] the Christ of God" (v. 20). His confession left his peers equally thrilled, and together they basked in the light of Jesus' glory. Their hearts overflowed with unspeakable wonder and their lips with joyful words as they considered just who He was—God Himself in the flesh with them.

But just then, in verses 22–26, Jesus brought them down with the sobering reality of His approaching appointment with the cross. Despite His deity, the Lamb of God had to be slain: "Saying, The Son of man must suffer many things, and be rejected by the elders and chief priests and scribes, and be slain" (v. 22). To this He added another heavy word. If they were to remain His disciples, they too must eventually accept their own crosses and follow Him in the way of Christian sufferings, or else fail their spiritual destiny: "And he said to them all, If any man will come after me, let him deny himself, and take up his cross daily, and follow me" (v. 23). This left them stunned, numb and silent with discouragement.

But Jesus didn't leave them comfortless very long. In verses 27–36, He took them up—to the summit of the Mount of Transfiguration: "And it came to pass, about eight days after these sayings, that he took Peter and John and James, and went up into a mountain to pray. And as he prayed, the |appearance| of his countenance was altered, and his raiment was white and |glistening|" (vv. 28–29). What His inner circle of apostles witnessed there was almost indescribable; indeed, it was a glimpse of Jesus' eternal glory and kingdom, virtually a visit to heaven. And the Lord wasn't finished yet, as we see in verses 37–42. After this high came another. The very day they descended from the mount, He displayed His divine power by delivering a demon-possessed boy: "And Jesus rebuked the unclean spirit, and healed the child, and delivered him again to his father" (v. 42). The impact of these unexpected favors—seeing Jesus' glory unveiled and His power displayed—left the disciples happily shocked: "And they were all |astonished| at the mighty power of God" (v. 43). Again, they were lifted up with intense religious excitement.

So, once again, Jesus brought them down by repeating

the sobering news of His upcoming sufferings: "But while they marveled every one at all things which Jesus did, he said unto his disciples, Let these sayings sink down into your ears; for the Son of man shall be delivered into the hands of men" (vv. 43–44). Make no mistake, this reality check wasn't what they wanted to hear, but it was exactly what they needed to hear. And it left them exactly the way He wanted them: humble, sober, clear-headed and spiritually alert, ready for the Master's use.

Luke 10

In verses 1–20, we find that Jesus continued His work of tempering, this time with the "other seventy also" (v. 1).

After returning from their first missionary trip (see verses 1–16), these anointed lay ministers were red hot with holy enthusiasm. Or so they thought. Their work had been a roaring success, and they roared about it in the Master's ears: "And the seventy returned again with joy, saying, Lord, even the |demons| are subject unto us through thy name" (v. 17). Ever sensitive to the Spirit, Jesus immediately detected something besides holy joy in their words—religious pride, to be specific. So, to remedy their overheated condition, He promptly threw a bucketful of cold words their way. Using Satan's fall as an example, He warned them of the subtle, often unnoticed danger of pride (v. 18) and urged them to rejoice henceforth in their relationship to Him, not in the work He enabled them to accomplish (vv. 19–20; see Jeremiah 9:23–24). Like the Twelve, the seventy were not thrilled by His correction, but they needed it and apparently wisely accepted it. In a matter of minutes, their spiritual temperatures were back to normal, thanks to the unerring discernment of the Temperer.

With divine precision, Jesus' words revealed their error. During and after their evangelistic crusade, they had become picked up with pride, apparently as they remembered, and so relived in imagination, their many successes. Obviously they failed to bring these self-centered, self-exalting thoughts into captivity to God's Word (as 2 Corinthians 10:3–5 states) and failed to give due praise to Him alone. As a result, they were joyful, but not for the right reasons. They did not rejoice that demonic captives had been freed, sinners reborn and saints' prayers answered. Nor were they thankful that God had made known His love by demonstrating His compassion for the sick and oppressed. They were not glad that Jesus' name had been glorified, His message broadcast and His kingdom eternally enlarged. No, none of these holy causes excited them. Instead, they were thrilled only by one narrow thought—*they* had spiritual power. Their words betray this, the true cause of their joy: "Lord, even the |demons| are subject unto *us* through thy name" (Luke 10:17, emphasis added). Hence, as always, the Temperer's corrective was perfectly timed.

It was just what they needed just when they needed it, a true word in season: "A word spoken in due season, how good is it!" (Prov. 15:23). It calmed them and enabled them to rethink their mission from the spiritual perspective. It was not their success; it was God's success through them. It was not their power; it was God's power given them in trust. It was not their glory; it was His glory. The demons were not bowing to them; they were bowing to Him. And their religious works, however earnest and blessed of God, didn't make them any more valuable to Jesus than they were before their mission. They had just done their Christian duty, as others had before them and others would after them. That's all. So the Temperer's goal was achieved in their souls.

And so these early Christian soldiers learned one of the greatest lessons of ministry: The battle is the Lord's—and the victory also.

116

THE TEMPERER'S WORK:
SPIRITUAL EXERCISE

As Jesus tempered His disciples, foremost in His mind was this great fact:

> Psychological and emotional exercises are just as real as physical exercise and achieve similar results. They firm up our souls, strengthen our spirits, sharpen our minds and increase our personal endurance, just as physical exercise strengthens and enlarges our muscles and increases our physical endurance.

Every joy and sorrow we pass through in fellowship with Jesus forces us to examine our attitudes and align them with God's viewpoint. When we're lifted up, we must confess the sin of pride (see 1 John 1:9) and humble ourselves; when we're disappointed and offended with God, we must confess this sin (see Luke 7:23) and choose to give thanks and reassume a scripturally positive attitude of trust, obedience and worship. If we don't, we quickly degenerate and are at risk of backsliding. This necessary soul effort exercises our spirits, emotions and minds. Hence, it hones our spiritual abilities and increases our spiritual stability and stamina. The result is that we more readily see our daily trials and triumphs from the spiritual perspective and so are much less likely to be moved by the varying highs and lows of life. In short, we become more spiritually mature. Alluding to this, the writer to the Hebrews described spiritually mature Christians as "those who by reason of use have their *senses exercised to discern* both good and evil" (Heb. 5:14, emphasis added). It was to instill this spiritual maturity that Jesus exercised His disciples' souls as described above.

This is why He heated them with revelations and then cooled them suddenly with warnings. This is why He took them high with visions and then sent them plunging downward with reproofs. This is why He enflamed them with demonstrations of His thrilling power and then doused them with unpleasant truths. The Master Temperer was at work. He used these soul exercises to make His disciples, especially His apostles, firm and tough, durable materials for an enduring work, just as a blacksmith "exercises" iron when shaping and tempering it for maximum strength. Repeatedly, Jesus put the apostles "through fire and through water" (Ps. 66:12), so every one of them would emerge from His forge "an instrument for his work" (Isa. 54:16). They had to be strong steel to lead, and so support, His temple, the church. Soft, untempered men would be unable to bear the load.

Was His tempering successful? The Book of Acts reveals that it was. The destructive forces the apostles constantly faced did not break them. They stood the heat of revival and the cold of persecution time and again without falling to pieces. Success did not make them giddy, nor did adversity discourage them. As tempered steel, they could not be broken, crushed or bent. Once established, they stood fast, as mighty pillars of righteousness. Noting their exceptional spiritual stability, Paul wrote, "James, Cephas [Peter], and John, *who seemed to be pillars*" (Gal. 2:9, emphasis added; see Ephesians 2:20). Their indefatigable strength inspired and upheld thousands of new converts during the days of their spiritual infancy, and their unmovable humility kept them close to Jesus, scripturally sound and sharp in spiritual discernment. From a human perspective, this was the reason for the miraculously rapid yet stable growth of the first-century church. Tempered leaders produce temperate churches.

THE TEMPERER WILL WORK

The Temperer still watches over Christians' souls today, constantly monitoring our psychological and emotional temperatures. By exposing us alternately to joys and sorrows, thrills and disappointments, prosperity and adversity, He tempers our souls just as He did His original followers. Why?

He seeks earnestly to bring us to the level of strength and consistency He requires for His End-Time work. As Isaiah declared, "I will strengthen and harden you [to difficulties]" (Isa. 41:10, AMP). He wants us to rise steadily from one level of spiritual strength to the next: "They go from strength to strength—increasing in victorious power" (Ps. 84:7, AMP). Although we often dislike it, we need this tempering. It alone gives us the strength to "run, and not be weary" and to "walk, and not faint" (Isa. 40:31). In a word, the difference between tempered and untempered Christians is *strength!* And strength is the difference between standing and shattering in the crisis. Natural tempering illustrates this.

Tempered glass is up to five times as strong as normal glass and can therefore withstand very strong blows without shattering. Tempered steel can bear extremely heavy burdens, pressures that would bend or break ordinary steel. Spiritual tempering creates similar results. Tempered Christians can take the shocks of sudden trouble and the heavy strains of prolonged crises without being knocked out of the race that is set before them. No matter what the enemy does against them, they endure and work on. Nothing moves them from close fellowship with Jesus, accurate spiritual discernment, courageous faith and steadfast service. The apostle Paul, a superbly tempered soul, authored the motto of tempered Christians: "None of these things move me" (Acts 20:24). Truly, no low has the power to offend tempered ones and no high renders them spiritually intoxicated and foolishly forgetful of God and duty. They can walk in the Spirit under any conditions, on solid land or surging waves. Therefore, God can and will use them in the construction of His works—churches, ministries, missions and spiritual movements. They will form the inner framework—the key supporting ministers and leaders—of His coming and final "habitation of God through the Spirit" (Eph.

119

2:22). And in Christ's kingdom, they will take their rightful place among others who submitted to His tempering until they learned to walk with Him consistently, beautifully unaffected by prosperity and adversity.

Can You See—Will You Submit to— the Work of the Temperer?

The next time life throws cold water on your red-hot religious excitement, hold your tongue before you blurt out, "It's the devil!" Remember this chapter, open the eyes of your spiritual understanding, and look and think again.

The devil may be standing before you holding the bucket, but Jesus has sent him: "This thing is from me" (1 Kings 12:24). There is something divine, not diabolical, at work. Your unforeseen, unexciting circumstances—delays, lulls, mundane activities, quiet days—are only doing the Lord's will. He is protecting you from falling by sending circumstances that keep you sober, sound and sure. He is training you to live on a steady emotional plane—not as an insensitive stoic, but as a spiritually consistent man or woman of God, scripturally minded, unmoved by religious fads, strong, predictable and dependable. Therefore, fully accept the circumstances He has ordained that He may fully temper you. And have faith—He will lift you up again just as surely as He has brought you low: "The Lord...[He] lifteth up" (1 Sam. 2:7). And consider the glorious end of your inglorious training. When fully tempered, you will absorb sharp blows without fainting and experience high success without becoming proud. As such, you will be fit to be a pillar in His church, one to whom others can look for spiritual support.

So change your confession. Loose your tongue and repeat these words in submissive faith: "It's the Temperer. He's at work in my soul. I will let Him do what seemeth to Him good."

And if this seems too unpleasant, you have an alternative. You can refuse to be tempered. But that will leave you spiritually weak and vulnerable to the strategy of the preemptor.

Chapter Thirteen

THE PREEMPTOR

The thief cometh not but to steal, and to kill, and to destroy.

—JOHN 10:10

The best time to stop something is before it starts. Once a work or movement gets underway, momentum builds, and its forward movement then becomes much harder to halt.

Satan obviously believes this, for as "the thief" he busies himself trying to stop God's works before they have a chance to begin. Christ taught, "The thief [Satan] cometh...to steal" (John 10:10). Now ordinary thieves wait until the spoil arrives, then sneak in to take it. But Satan is no ordinary thief. He is way ahead of his typical Christian victim. Well before the arrival of the thing he plans to steal, he's hard at work resisting, spoiling and destroying. Satan is, therefore, the preemptor.

123

According to *Webster's New World College Dictionary*, to preempt is "to seize before anyone else can"; preemption is "action taken [beforehand] to check other action." Practically speaking, preemption is doing something before someone else does it and thereby preventing them from doing it. For example, realizing that a competitor plans to buy a prime piece of real estate and use it to put him out of business, the shrewd businessman simply acts first. He buys the property himself, thus preventing his rival from doing so. What has he done? He has preempted his competitor. He has defeated his rival's plan while it's still on the drawing board, well in advance of its implementation. He has crushed his adversary's vision before he could even begin to fulfill it.

Our adversary, the devil, is equally shrewd. He has an uncanny ability to detect when, where and through whom God is about to act to bless people and glorify Himself. Sensing this, the devil moves first, hoping to kill the blessing in the womb, to "steal, and to kill, and to destroy" God's work before it is born into manifestation. He knows well that if you prevent a tree from being planted, it will never bear fruit. He understands that if you uproot seeds, they will never produce a harvest. He realizes that if a foundation is not laid, a superstructure cannot be built and used. And more importantly, he recognizes that if God's work never begins, it can't be finished. And if God's work isn't finished, it can't bring Him glory, for God is glorified only when we finish His work. While the devil's comprehension of the spirit of Scripture is debatable, his grasp of its letter is not; he has surely read Jesus' High Priestly prayer and noted the obvious link between the words "glorified thee" and "finished the work": "I have glorified thee...I have finished the work which thou gavest me to do" (John 17:4). Hence, knowing that every divinely ordered work carried through to completion glorifies God, and driven to deprive God of such glory,

Satan's strategy against every work of God is simple: Stop it before it starts! Have we ever detected this strategy at work?

So often we see the enemy coming with counterblows, attacking saints after they have attacked his kingdom. Peter and John's preaching resulted in thousands being saved in the temple courts; immediately the Jewish leaders appeared, arrested them and put them in jail. (See Acts 3–4.) Paul cast a demon out of a Philippian fortuneteller; immediately her masters had him beaten and jailed without a trial. (See Acts 16.) Stephen's faith produced great miracles in Jerusalem; immediately the Libertines began contending with him and delivered him to the Sanhedrin for official condemnation. (See Acts 6–7.) We are very familiar with this kind of back-and-forth, blow-for-blow spiritual warfare. But Satan's work as the preemptor is different.

THE PREEMPTOR'S WORK: ANTICIPATORY PERSECUTION

As the preemptor, Satan practices *anticipatory persecution,* or satanic opposition that anticipates or precedes the divine work it opposes. Whenever God initiates a spiritual movement to bless His people, Satan doesn't sit by idly until the movement is in full progress and then attack it. He always tries to prevent its beginning—to destroy God's ark before it is launched; to clip the wings of God's eagles before they mount up, soar and take prey; to snuff out spiritual fire before it breaks out. He sometimes strikes so early that we don't even realize what he's after until his attack has passed. For instance, he tries to separate us from our close Christian friends; then we realize that such friendships are God's foundation for a fellowship, church or ministry. He disrupts our ministry; then we recognize that the "precious seed" we are sowing is creating a potentially vast spiritual harvest in many lives. He tries to uproot us from our church; then we realize that the sound

125

teaching we're receiving there is rooting us deeply in God and making us trees planted by rivers of water that will bring forth fruit in due season. (See Psalm 1:1–3.) Then it hits us: How slow we are—and how quick the enemy is—to recognize spiritual potential! Yet this really shouldn't surprise us. From the beginning of time, the enemy has been trying to obstruct God's work.

Throughout Scripture the preemptor's distinct footprints are evident:

- Satan tried to preempt the Exodus by prompting Pharaoh to kill Israel's newborn males just when Moses, God's predestined deliverer, was to be born. (See Acts 7:19–20.) He knew well that to kill the deliverer is to kill the deliverance.

- Satan tried to prevent God's redemption by prompting Herod to slaughter the young males of Bethlehem (Matt. 2:16–18). If the Savior had died in the cradle, He couldn't have saved us on the cross.

- The enemy attempted to keep the gospel from the Gentiles by inspiring a death plot against Saul, who as the apostle Paul would become God's primary spokesman to the Gentiles. (See Acts 9:23.) This plot was hatched long before God sent Saul on his first mission. If Saul's light had been extinguished in Damascus, "the apostle of the Gentiles" (Rom. 11:13) would never have illuminated entire regions of the world, including Caesar's household.

- Satan perceived that through Hannah would come the mighty prophet Samuel, and through him, spiritual revival to all Israel. So he inspired Peninnah to vex Hannah relentlessly for many years, hoping to prevent Samuel's birth. (See 1 Samuel 1:1–8.) If Hannah had succumbed to this persecution, she would have remained without child—and Israel without revival.

- As Solomon's coronation drew near, Adonijah suddenly made a bold claim upon Israel's throne (1 Kings 1:1–53). Why did his previously dormant ambition arise at just that time? Because his inspirer, Satan, hoped to end Israel's greatest period of prosperity and prominence before it began. If Adonijah had reigned, the world would never have witnessed "Solomon, in all his glory" (Matt. 6:29).

- Adonijah's coup foreshadows the rise of Antichrist, through whose brief world rule Satan will attempt to preempt the glorious millennial reign of Christ. Just when the time draws near for God's Son to return to Jerusalem to rule all nations, Satan will send his "son," Antichrist, to seize Jerusalem and rule all nations from that very place. If God were to permit Antichrist's kingdom to continue, the world's government would never rest upon Christ's shoulders.

Recent history reveals the preemptor's diabolical work:

- The Holocaust was more than Hitler's mad quest. It was Satan's attempt to prevent Zionism (a worldwide movement to reestablish a Jewish state in Palestine) from restoring the nation of Israel—a long-awaited fulfillment of Bible prophecy (1948) and a key to the fulfillment of all End-Time prophecies. Sensing that the Jews' regathering was near, Satan inspired Hitler's attempted genocide, hoping to block the Jews' physical reunion in Palestine and, more importantly, to preempt their future spiritual conversion en masse (after the rapture of the church), a miraculous national rebirth that will spawn a worldwide revival during the first half of the Tribulation period.

(See Romans 11:25–26; Revelation 7:1–17.)

Exactly how the enemy is able to anticipate God's actions is not revealed in Scripture, but that he does so is evident. In the examples cited above, Satan sensed *when* God was about to act and began his opposition just before God's appointed hour arrived. He sensed *where* God was going to move and directed his attack against that city or that nation. And he sensed *through whom* God was going to act and poured great afflictions upon those very people—God's chosen servants—long before God's powerful hand rested upon them for His purpose.

Do You Wonder, Why Me, Lord?

When our lives seem outwardly barren and unimportant, and yet we find ourselves persistently harassed by Satan as if we were prominent and fruitful, we may wonder, and even pray, *Why me, Lord?* David experienced this.

When David was a teenager, the Philistines made war against Israel, and their giant, Goliath, emerged and defied Israel's army. (See 1 Samuel 17.) Since David's three oldest brothers had enlisted, David's father, Jesse, sent him to Israel's war camp to see if his brothers were still alive (vv. 17–29). When he arrived, David heard Goliath's bold challenge and promptly suggested that someone respond (v. 26). Just then, his oldest brother, Eliab, interrupted and angrily reproached David, accusing his humble and obedient sibling of being a proud and curious interferer (v. 28). Struck by the unreasonableness of Eliab's offensive outburst, David said, "What have I now done? Is there not a cause?" (v. 29). Indeed, there was a cause, and it was twofold. First, from a natural viewpoint, Eliab was apparently envious of David, whom the Lord had chosen to become Israel's next king despite Samuel's initial preference for Eliab. (See 1 Samuel 16:6–13.) Second, from a spiritual perspective, Satan was using Eliab's envy as a channel through which he hoped to offend David and so prevent his impending exploit against Goliath, which glorified God greatly.

Have you, as David, found yourself on the receiving end of unreasonable opposition and wondered, *What have I now done? Is there not a cause?* Your "cause" may be that the enemy is trying to derail God's glorious plan for your future in Christ. You may be predestined to defeat a Goliath or occupy an office through which God will greatly bless His people and glorify His name. Remember, the preemptor's resistance manifests *before* God's full-blown purpose for our lives is evident. Hence, satanic opposition appears before we see its divine cause. Hannah, for instance, was still barren while Peninnah was harassing her to tears; later she gave birth to the mighty prophet Samuel. Joseph had not interpreted any dreams when his brothers threw him into a pit; later his prophetic ministry saved the world. Moses had delivered no one from Egypt, not even himself, at the time the Hebrews rejected him, saying, "Who made thee a ruler and a judge over us?" (Acts 7:27); later he delivered his nation from bondage. Clearly, all these souls bore a cross in the present because they would bear glory in the future. So take heart.

The opposition that has pursued and sometimes overwhelmed you in obscurity may be the work of the preemptor and evidence that you too are chosen by God to one day blossom and bear much fruit. Satan may be trying to disrupt the very effective training process in which you are presently engaged, knowing that if your training is cut short, your eventual ministry will be prevented or limited. (See chapter 1, pages 5–7.) If you are sure God has called you, don't presume anything. Be fully obedient to the heavenly vision: "I was not disobedient unto the heavenly vision" (Acts 26:19). Diligently prepare yourself to fulfill your calling. Listen carefully and learn your lessons well in the darkness that Jesus may bring you forth to speak in the light. (See Matthew 10:27.) In every way do your part to become fit for the Master's use. Then, despite the preemptor's worst, your best—your finest hour in Christ—is sure to come.

On the other hand, you may already be in God's work. If you are being viciously attacked just as fruitful ministry opportunities are opening up, satanic preemption may also explain your problem. Courtesy of the preemptor, enemies always rush in to prevent the opening of effective doors of ministry. (See chapter 1, pages 7–9.) The apostle Paul recognized that for every "great door" that is "effectual" there are "many adversaries": "For a great door, and effectual, is opened unto me, and there are many adversaries" (1 Cor. 16:9). At Ziklag, the preemptor tried to crush David with discouragement just as his forty-year kingship—a great and effectual door indeed—was about to begin. The motive of the attack certainly wasn't David's current fruitfulness, for at the time David was a fugitive in exile, utterly defamed. He hadn't produced any tangible fruit for God in more than a decade. It was the abundant fruit David was yet to bear during his upcoming reign—Israel's national deliverance (from Philistine oppression), unprecedented national righteousness, peace and security—that the enemy hoped to spoil. Additionally, he also hoped to block David's lifelong ministry as Israel's worship leader and his endless ministry as the church's (yes, the world's) inspired psalmist.

~

So, friend, if the preemptor is after you, rejoice. Your life may not be pleasant now, but it's promising. God will one day reap much fruit and glory from you if you will just remain faithful—that is, learn to hold on when your circumstantial "boat" is overflowing with troubled waters.

Chapter Fourteen

IS YOUR
BOAT FULL?

And there arose a great storm of wind, and the waves
beat into the |boat|, so that it was now full.

—MARK 4:37

Shortly after the apostles embarked on their first-recorded
crossing of the Sea of Galilee, a storm arose. (See Mark
4:35–41.) This was no minor squall; it was a "great" storm (v.
37). The Amplified Bible describes it as "a furious storm of
wind (of hurricane proportions)." As if the fury and confusion
of the storm were not terrifying enough to the apostles, more
trouble arose: The waves began to "beat into the |boat|" (v.
37), and the small, open-hull vessel began taking on water. And
as if this tribulation were insufficient to try their faith, their
condition continued getting worse: The waves kept pounding
into the boat until it was on the verge of sinking: "It was now
full" (v. 37). Thus, the situation into which Jesus had guided

them (their boat) was filled with troubled waters—literally!

Does this reflect your present situation? Is your boat—the situation into which the Lord has led you—now *full*, or swamped with overwhelming troubles? Are serious problems pressing in from all sides at the same time with no solutions in sight? Do you feel somewhat like Paul, who wrote, "We were pressed out of measure, above strength, insomuch that we despaired even of life" (2 Cor. 1:8)? (See also 2 Corinthians 4:8–10, 17–18.) Despite this fullness of trouble, are new griefs and sorrows, as waves, continuing to crash in upon your already overburdened heart? Has this merciless buffeting continued longer than you or anyone else anticipated, longer than you thought you could bear? If so, take heed and take heart, because Mark 4:35–41 contains good news for you.

A MODEL TEST FILLED WITH SPIRITUAL PATTERNS

Mark 4:35–41 is a description of a model test. As such, it gives us several unfailing patterns of spiritual action.

First, this story reveals a pattern of divine action—what we may expect God to do in our tests. Just as Jesus slept and then awakened to deliver His disciples, so God also may seem asleep (silent, inactive and unconcerned) in our trials, yet in reality He remains ever faithful to "awake," or intervene, and make a way of escape if we but trust and obey Him. Second, it reveals a pattern of satanic action—what we may expect Satan to do in our tests. As the winds stirred the waves that troubled the apostles' boat, so Satan's invisible agents—the "power[s] of the air" (Eph. 2:2)—stir the people and problems that press and buffet our lives. Like these winds and waves, Satan's agents are relentless. Third, it reveals patterns of human action—things we should and should not do in our trials. Just as the apostles' prayer-cry—albeit agitated—prompted Jesus to terminate their stormy test, so also we should seek a divine release from our trials through prayer, but we should not succumb to unbelief, murmuring and panic as they did.

THE SYMBOLISM

There is rich symbolism in this passage. As mentioned earlier, the apostles followed Jesus into their boat. (See Matthew 8:23.) Once there, their faith in Him was tested. Thus, their boat represents the situations into which the Lord leads us for the purposes of spiritual testing. Besides being apostles, the Twelve were also Jesus' disciples. Hence, they represent Christian disciples, who, like the Twelve, are called to follow Jesus daily. (See Romans 8:14.) The apostles' test occurred in the evening (Mark 4:35), after they had spent a full day receiving Jesus' teachings. (See Mark 4:1–34.) Our evening is the God-ordained season of trial we meet once we are well taught in God's Word. (Tribulation or persecution always comes because of hearing the Word; see Matthew 13:21.) The apostles' boat was battered by a "great storm of wind" (Mark 4:37) and the agitating waves it stirred. This speaks of demonic forces gathering and attacking us with especially strong resistance and trouble intended to terminate our faith and fruitfulness in Christ. When He called the apostles to their brief but turbulent crossing, Jesus described their destination as the "other side" of the lake (v. 35) or, as Mark states, the "country of the Gerasenes" (Mark 5:1). There they assisted Him as He performed an extraordinarily powerful deliverance (vv. 2–16), which won Him fame throughout the region (v. 20). Our "other side" represents the end of our season of strong testing after which we too enter a new season of powerful service that will glorify the name of Jesus.

THE STORY UNFOLDS

After a peaceful launch (Mark 4:35), the apostles came under increasing pressure until at last they reached the point of the impossible. At that alarming moment their situation was undeniably desperate. The storm was "great," the waves were "beat[ing] into the |boat|," and the boat was "now full" (v. 37)—and Jesus, their all-powerful, compassionate Savior, was . . . well, asleep! "He was in the |stern| of the |boat|, *asleep* on a pillow" (v. 38, emphasis added). Incredible as it may seem, the ultimate Helper wasn't doing anything to help His own. He was neither giving the apostles instructions, nor exhorting them, nor bailing water. He wasn't even praying! Just sleeping. What a time for a nap!

Just then—when the apostles realized the full extent of their trouble and of Jesus' apparent indifference—they reached the spiritual "break point" in their trial, which is the crucial moment that determines victory or defeat. And, unfortunately, they broke; that is, their faith lapsed. Offended and angry with their Master, they awakened Him with a panic prayer laced with accusations and unbelief: "Master, carest thou not that we perish?" (v. 38). Graciously, the Lord arose and delivered them. Then, justly, He rebuked them: "Why are ye so fearful? How is it that ye have no faith?" (v. 40). Hence, delivered but dissatisfied with themselves, "they came over unto the other side of the sea" (Mark 5:1).

THE REASON FOR THE APOSTLES' FAILURE

Succinctly, panic was the reason the apostles failed their test of faith. But panic doesn't just happen. It is an effect arising from clearly identifiable previous causes.

In the apostles' case, they panicked because they forgot the spiritual facts they knew and focused instead on the natural facts surrounding them. When sorely tried, overcoming believers keep the facts of faith in full focus and the discouraging facts of actual circumstances in their peripheral (side) vision. But the apostles had not yet learned to discipline their heart-vision. So under the extreme pressure of the storm, their faith lapsed. A clear sequence of events led to their lapse.

First, as already stated, they focused on the things seen. By doing so, they completely forgot the vital facts of their faith, which they already knew well. These facts were:

1. His PRESENCE. Jesus was with them bodily in the boat. Despite the pressure, they had the presence. Water or no water, "he was in the |boat|" (Mark 4:36; see 4:38). Hence, they were safe. (See Psalm 46:1–3; Isaiah 41:10; 43:1–2.)

2. His PROMISE. Jesus had personally led them into the boat and had clearly promised they would arrive at the "other side" (Mark 4:35). Hence, they were in God's will and had His promise.

3. His POWER. Jesus was a miracle worker and could easily do the impossible at any moment; they had personally seen Him perform countless miracles. (See Mark 3:7–12.) Hence, supernatural—yes, almighty—help was on their side.[1]

As these faithful facts faded from their minds, lying fears rushed in in their stead. Their exact fears were betrayed by their words. First, they believed Jesus didn't care about them any more: "Master, *carest* thou not?" (Mark 4:38, emphasis added). Second, they were convinced that this was the end for them. Surely they would breathe their last in this ferocious storm: "We *perish*" (v. 38, emphasis added). Because they failed to recognize the satanic origin of these fears (see 2 Timothy 1:7) and immediately cast them down, unbelief and offense set in. It was all over then. Within moments, fear overwhelmed them, and they started shouting panic prayers at the Lord.

Despite the apostles' failure, this model test and its symbolism reveal several sound scriptural reasons why we should remain optimistic when our God-ordained circumstances are full of troubles.

REASONS FOR OPTIMISM
WHEN YOUR BOAT IS FULL

Things can't get worse

When the apostles' boat became "now full," their adversity had maxed out. Only sinking could have been worse, and that wasn't possible because Jesus was in their boat. (Even the *Titanic* would have remained afloat had He been one of its occupants!) So from this point until their trial's end, their stress did not increase. And in their condition, that was a blessing.

You too can thank the Lord when your Christ-appointed trials become full of trouble. Because your boat's (situation's) capacity is *filled*, additional waters (troubles) can't get in. They just flow over the top: "All thy billows and thy waves passed over me" (Jon. 2:3; see Psalm 69:1–2, 14–15). So rejoice: Your test can't get any worse. Satan can't hit you with anything new because he's already hit you with everything he's got. There's nothing left to dread, even if you wanted to! When you reach this "miracle or sink" point, things can only improve. You've reached that dreadful yet promising destination: spiritual rock bottom. Your cycle of adversity has reached its end, and a new cycle of prosperity is at hand. As with Joseph in prison and David at Ziklag, the only way to go now is *up!*

A sign of imminent intervention

The filling of the apostles' boat with water was the last adverse event recorded before their sudden release. So intense and wild was that stress-crazed fullness of trouble that it seemed as if it would never end. Deceptively, it offered no hint that a totally opposite scenario—a peaceful, stress-free Galilee—was only moments away. But it was. The apostles' deliverance was near. Very near. The next thing we read is that after the apostles' agitated cry, Jesus finally did something about their situation: "And he arose, and rebuked the wind, and said unto the sea, Peace, be still" (Mark 4:39). And suddenly, when moments earlier the storm looked as if it would never end, it was all over: "And the wind ceased" (v. 39). So the boat's fullness was a subtle sign that Jesus' intervention was at hand.

When your heart is overwhelmed with surging perplexities and multiple waves of distress, and you feel so full of grief you cannot speak, remember this model test and be encouraged; it's time for the Lord to intervene and help you. "The coming of the Lord draweth |near|" (James 5:8). Very soon Jesus will "awake" from His silence and inactivity and begin commanding and creating an overruling peace upon your overwhelming trial. And suddenly, though it seemed it would never end, your anguish will cease.

A "great calm" is coming

After Jesus intervened, a "great calm" settled in upon the exhausted apostles and their previously agitated boat: "And there was a great calm" (Mark 4:39). Note that the degree of their newfound tranquility was equal to that of their former distress; both their storm and their peace were "great" (vv. 37, 39). For enduring great turmoil they were rewarded with great peace. This wasn't the only time this happened to Christ's servants. After Paul was tossed about by a fierce Mediterranean storm for over two weeks and nearly killed in a violent shipwreck, the Lord gave him three long months of peace and quiet and joyful ministry on the island of Malta. (See Acts 28:1–11.) For him too it was a "great calm" following a great storm.

Are you in a "great storm" today? If your boat is very full, you may take comfort in knowing that *the stronger the storm, the deeper the peace God gives when He delivers.* The more severe and confused your trauma, the clearer and quieter will be its end. So praise the Lord! He will recompense you fully for the agitation you are now experiencing. Look up in anticipation of your "great calm."

You will gain a new fear of the Lord

The magnitude of Jesus' intervention left its mark upon His apostles. As never before, they realized that He was very God of very God—not just an exceptionally gifted prophet. All Jesus' previous miracles paled in light of this one. Healing the sick and the lame and casting out demons were certainly acts of supernatural power, but commanding the very forces of nature—that topped them all! Only the Creator could control the creation's most basic elements of earth, wind and fire. Was this He? Oh, they wondered! "And they feared exceedingly, and said one to another, What manner of man is this, that even the wind and the sea obey him?" (Mark 4:41). Thus, suddenly, a new and even greater "fear of the Lord"—respect for Jesus' power and warnings—gripped their hearts. And it never left them, even unto martyrdom. Henceforth, they chose consistently to displease governors, high priests and kings, if necessary, but not Him!

When you see the Lord supernaturally release you from the jaws of death, suddenly you too will be awestruck by His power. And you will live your remaining days in a new dimension of the fear of the Lord. Never again will you resist His will, ignore His words or take His warnings lightly.

A deeper knowledge—and faith—will be yours

Before this turbulent episode, the apostles knew Jesus personally and believed in Him passionately. In fact, their knowledge of and faith in Him far surpassed that of other Israelites. Nevertheless, this experience deepened their knowledge and increased their faith.

Never before had the apostles reached a "panic point" such as the one they experienced in this storm. Previously, Jesus had kept them from intense trials. But here He pushed their faith to its limit that He might increase it. And never before had Jesus slept in the midst of serious trouble, apparently indifferent to His followers' welfare. Always His way was to respond in compassionate haste. So truly this trial was a new thing, and, as with all new experiences, it left the apostles temporarily shaken and confused. Yet by trial's end, they could look back and see what Jesus had done and why. He had withheld immediate assistance only to test their faith in His character: Would they still trust in His goodness and faithfulness when every fact reported that they were dying and He didn't care? The test would—and did—tell.

Even though they failed in this test, they were better disciples for having passed through it. The next time they encountered such extreme difficulties, they understood that their mounting problems were not due to Jesus' lack of power or compassion; instead, they were meant to give them an opportunity to trust His character and believe in His power and promises even when all hope seems lost. This understanding caused them to know Him more deeply. Before this stormy episode they knew His acts only; now they knew His character—utter faithfulness. (See 1 Corinthians 10:13; Hebrews 11:11.) Hence, they trusted Him more firmly. So because their knowledge of Him was deeper, their faith was stronger; and because their faith was stronger, their spiritual endurance was greater. They could now walk calmly with Jesus *beyond* the crucial "break point," which they did in the following trials of Jairus and Lazarus. (See Mark 5:22–24, 35–43; John 11:1–44.) Their experiences may explain yours.

If your boat is "now full" and neither calm seas nor land are in sight, it may be that Jesus wants you to trust not merely His power but His person. Manifestations of His power may vary, but His character never varies; it is gloriously unchanging. He wants you so deeply rooted and grounded in trust in His character that you never again panic. So look up: A new revelation of the character of Jesus and a much stronger faith in Him await you on the "other side" (Mark 4:35) of your current tribulation.

AN EXAMPLE *NOT* TO FOLLOW

As in some other Gospel references, the apostles in their watery boat set an example for us *not* to follow. Why? Because in the heat of trial they lost their heads. As stated earlier, they completely forgot Jesus' promise, presence and power, and they focused instead on their immediate troubles, namely, the howling storm and their troubled, sinking boat. Then, offended, they fell apart, assaulting Jesus with wild, hasty prayer-demands and hostile accusations that He, the infinitely good and faithful One, had failed them!

If they had only sat still a little longer, trusting in Jesus and calling on Him calmly and confidently for help, Jesus would have awakened and rebuked the storm. And instead of reprimanding them for fear, He would have commended them for relying on Him. Moreover, their faith would have been proven and their joy made full.

AN EXAMPLE TO FOLLOW— REVERSING THE APOSTLES' ERRORS

Failure becomes success when those who fail reverse their errors. With this in mind, let's reexamine this lesson.

To avoid repeating the apostles' failure in your stormy days, simply reverse their errors. When you reach your panic point—when the things seen tell you that your ship is sinking fast, that disaster, not landfall, is imminent—*refuse* to panic. Do not allow devastating fears to enter and control your mind; cast down every imagination and high thing that exalts itself against your faith. (See 2 Corinthians 10:3–5.) Then refill your mind with the Spirit by recalling the vital facts of your faith. Remember that:

- Jesus led you into your troubled "boat"; will He destroy those whom He leads?

- Jesus is with you; do you think He plans to go down

with your ship?

- Jesus has promised to take you to the "other side"; is He a man of His word or "a man, that He should lie"? (See Numbers 23:19.)

- Jesus is all-powerful; can the powers of the air, however ferocious, overpower the very Creator?

Also, since God is the God of all truth, recall other truths that stir your spirit and challenge you to overcome. Ponder memorable quotations from the great thinkers and writers of history, such as these excerpts from Rudyard Kipling's inspired poem "If":

If you can keep your head when all about you
    Are losing theirs and blaming it on you;
If you can trust yourself when all men doubt you,
    But make allowance for their doubting too;
If you can wait and not be tired by waiting,
    Or, being lied about, don't deal in lies,
Or, being hated, don't give way to hating,...

...If you can meet with triumph and disaster
    And treat those two impostors just the same;
If you can bear to hear the truth you've spoken
    Twisted by knaves to make a trap for fools...

...If you can force your heart and nerve and sinew
    To serve your turn long after they are gone,
And so hold on when there is nothing in you
    Except the Will which says to them: "Hold on";

...If you can fill the unforgiving minute
    With sixty seconds' worth of distance run—
Yours is the Earth and everything that's in it,
    And—which is more—you'll be a Man, my son![2]

Furthermore, ponder at length the infallible word-portrait

141

the Spirit paints for us in Mark 4:35–41. There we see Jesus and His faithful ones stranded in a boat that should be sinking, yet it is still floating. Translated, this tells us that Jesus Christ has the unique ability to keep flooded boats—and overburdened souls—above water if their occupants will only keep trusting Him. Then believe and apply this message. If the Lord has given you His Word of promise, no matter how frightening and contradictory the facts of your immediate storm, choose to trust Him and wait for His intervention. "Be still, and know" (Ps. 46:10) that He can easily overrule whatever or whomever is presently overruling you. Or as the songwriter put it:

> Be still, my soul—thy God doth undertake,
> To guide the future as He has the past;
> Thy hope, thy confidence let nothing shake,
> All now mysterious shall be bright at last.
> Be still, my soul—the waves and winds still know,
> His voice who ruled them while He dwelt below.[3]

Finally, do what the apostles failed to do at the break point in their trial—fervently but calmly ask the Lord to awake, arise and deliver you. And continue doing so daily—without offense or panic—until He does it. (See Luke 18:1.)

If You Will...

If you will thus endure, your endurance will bless God greatly. He is overjoyed when His children deliberately wait for heaven-sent help in the midst of earthly chaos. Nothing satisfies His heart more than our persevering patience amid the panicky perplexities of life. And those who bless Him, He will bless.

First, He will grant you all the previously stated benefits: You will receive a new peace; the fear of the Lord will rest more heavily upon you; you will gain a deeper knowledge of God; your faith will become much stronger and your endurance greater. Second, He will release you from your immediate storm; you will reach your "other side." Third, instead of rebuking you for your fear, He will commend your trust and patience. Fourth, your proven-by-deeds faith will become your "ticket for translation." It will qualify you to escape the entire Tribulation period, that greatest of storms set to descend upon the sea of humanity after the rapture of the church. Jesus promised, "Because thou hast kept the word of my patience, I also will keep thee from the hour of temptation, which shall come upon all the world, to try them that dwell upon the earth" (Rev. 3:10). Fifth, your example will inspire many other Christians, and the Lord will call them to follow your faith; as the psalmist declared, "Many shall see it [your deliverance], and fear, and shall trust in the LORD" (Ps. 40:3).

~

So stand steady by praying steadily. Avoid panic prayers by maintaining your private fellowship with Jesus and offering powerful prayers—calm, confident petitions accompanied by worship, thanksgiving, recitations of God's promises and confessions of faith in His unfailing character and Word. Then protect your stand by watching.

Watch out for self-pity. When it presses in, remember you're not alone. Others are being tested just as severely as you. During the apostles' ordeal, "there were also with him [and them] other little |boats|" (Mark 4:36). God has many other little groups of believers just like yours—true, troubled, but triumphant. While it is accurate to say that misery loves company, it is equally true that company relieves misery. So think and pray about your brethren, too, not just yourself.

Also, watch for panic. When you're weak and tempted to take matters into your hands, remind yourself that any attempt to create your own way of escape will only bring more trouble and, if persisted in, disaster. (See chapter 17.) When the apostle Paul saw panicky sailors preparing to jump ship in the midst of a hurricane, he exhorted their captain, "Except these abide in the ship, ye cannot be saved" (Acts 27:31). Stirred by his wise word, they remained aboard and were soon delivered. Here's another stirring word: Because your circumstantial "boat" is God's will for you, despite all its troubles, it is the safest place you can be right now. So stay there.

And if you need extra motivation, remember how suddenly the apostles' trial ended. Believe that your deliverance, when it comes, will be just as sudden. In a moment, everything will change. In the brilliant biography *Elijah and the Secret of His Power*, F. B. Meyer wrote:

> When men have done their worst and finished, it is the time for God to begin. And when God begins He is likely, with one blow, to reverse all that has been done without Him.[4]

So although your storm is great and your boat is full, keep hope alive. Who knows when your "one blow" may come and suddenly bring you, stunned but joyful, to the shores of a calm, new day of powerful service? That is, unless God forgets about you and your troubled little "ark."

Chapter Fifteen

HAS THE LORD
FORGOTTEN YOU?

And God remembered Noah…

—GENESIS 8:1

A t precisely the midpoint of the biblical account of the great flood we read these words: "And God remembered Noah" (Gen. 8:1). At its first reading this statement seems rather strange. The word *remembered*, as it is normally used, implies that someone or something has been forgotten. Had God indeed forgotten Noah, who at the time had been confined to the ark for five months? Did the Omniscient One suffer a memory lapse while the waters of judgment prevailed upon the face of the earth? We could understand if He had forgotten the wicked antediluvians (pre-flood populace). Stubbornly, they perished because they refused to receive the love of the truth and be saved. Truly, they were unworthy of

God's memory. But not Noah. He was God's best, His very man of the hour. Surely God didn't forget Noah? Consider this summary of biblical facts.

ABOUT THE MAN NOAH

So corrupt was the pre-flood world that only two souls, Enoch and Noah, "found grace" (Gen. 6:8) in God's sight and subsequently believed and walked in His ways. (See Genesis 5:21–24.) And after Enoch's translation, that tiny righteous remnant was further reduced to one. From then on, only Noah "walked with God" (Gen. 6:9) in a godless world. Among the vast number of antediluvians, only Noah believed the Lord and, in holy fear, obeyed His voice whenever He spoke. (See Hebrews 11:7.) He was also the only "preacher of righteousness" (2 Pet. 2:5); no one else urged lost souls to get right with God. And he was the only remaining prophet; only Noah had revelation concerning the approaching catastrophe. Moreover, he was God's only remaining servant; hence God commissioned him alone to build the ark. Furthermore, he pastored the only "church"—a vast throng of eight redeemed ones, including the preacher!—whose members were all in his extended family. (And you thought your church was small!) (See chapter 5.) Though tiny, Noah's called-out assembly was the only one to survive the deluge. Quite literally, then, God had invested *everything* in Noah and his little band of believers—the continuance of all life forms, humans, animals and plants; the preservation of the godly line, which began with Abel; the eventual creation of the chosen people of Israel, who descended from Noah; the coming of the Savior, who was an Israelite; and the Savior's work of redeeming the creation and establishing the church, in which millions, including you and me, now find refuge from the ongoing flood of sin and judgment. With all this at stake, heaven's eyes were surely fixed upon Noah. Angels probably jostled for the best seats as they peered earthward with unbroken concentration to see every fascinating event unfold in the drama of the ark.

WAS NOAH FORGOTTEN?

Yet, strangely, the wording of the Genesis narrative suggests just the opposite, that God had forgotten Noah's buffeted boat and its traumatized captain and occupants. Was this the case? Was celestial activity so great, or the divine work load so heavy, or God's grief over the death of millions so overwhelming that He was totally distracted during the one hundred fifty days following Noah's entry into the ark?

Certainly not. God didn't forget Noah for one second. When inspiring the Book of Genesis, the Holy Spirit led Moses to use the word *remembered* (Gen. 8:1, Hebrew *zakar*), not to imply divine forgetfulness, but to convey *Noah's* viewpoint. The statement reveals Noah's thoughts, not God's. In short, Noah *felt* as if God had forgotten him. And with good reason—for five months God had been totally silent and inactive from Noah's point of view. God had not spoken a single word to Noah; not once did Noah hear the Comforter's warm voice reassuring his lonely heart. Nor had God granted Noah any encouraging signs. During the long, gloomy period of rain, isolation, darkness and death, heaven gave no hints of the joyous process of deliverance that was approaching. Furthermore, God had done nothing to assist Noah; He had not committed a single act to help Noah escape his troubled waters. As a human being, therefore, Noah felt abandoned by God. And every new day seemed to further confirm his sinking feelings. For one hundred and fifty consecutive days, conditions grew worse by the hour.

NOAH'S TEST: A TIME OF RISING WATERS

First, the floodgates of both heavenly and subterranean water sources were flung open and a monsoon of unimaginable proportions ensued. For forty days and nights massive rains battered the ark with maddening constancy. (See Genesis 7:11–17.) After this initial assault ended, the rains of heaven and the springs of earth continued to release their troubled waters intermittently for three and a half more months. With every new cloudburst the waters rose ever higher. (See 7:18–24.) During this time of unrelieved darkness, despair and death, it may well have seemed to Noah that the God who ordered him into the ark had since fallen into a deep sleep. And, as stated earlier concerning Jesus' mid-storm nap (see chapter 14, pages 133–134), this was no time for slumber. If God didn't "awake" and stop the rising waters, Noah—and humanity with him—would perish.

But heaven's apparent indifference was meant to test, not terminate, Noah. While the flood was a judgment to the world, it was a grand trial of faith to Noah, his opportunity to prove and confirm his trust in God's character and His promises. God had promised Noah that the overwhelming flood would come—"And, behold, I, even I, do bring a flood of waters upon the earth, to destroy all flesh" (Gen. 6:17)—and it had. Furthermore, God had promised to establish His covenant with Noah (v. 18), plainly implying that one day the flood would end and Noah would resume his normal life on earth. Yet during his five months of rising waters Noah saw not even the slightest indication of an approaching end. So both Noah's faith and his very soul were tried. As was later true of Joseph, "until the time that his word came [was fulfilled]; the word of the LORD |tested| him" (Ps. 105:19). The crux of Noah's trial was simple: God had promised that his trial would end...but would it? Though Noah's innermost thoughts are not given us, it's likely that he was grateful the ark had delivered his family from the *flood*, but the lengthy trial must have made him wonder: When would they be delivered from the *ark?*

GOD "REMEMBERS" NOAH—
BY ACTS, SIGNS AND WORDS

Five months was the time limit God set on Noah's trial. When that juncture was reached, God immediately "remembered" Noah. That is:

HE BEGAN TO ACT AGAIN IN
NOAH'S BEHALF, SPEAKING AND GIVING
SIGNS OF FAVOR, AFTER A LONG PERIOD
OF INACTIVITY AND SILENCE.

Bursting forth from His celestial hiding place, the invisible God showed Himself throughout the earth as the God of Noah. Note the following specific acts, signs and words by which God encouraged His servant. His acts led the way.

His acts

First, the Lord caused a steady wind to blow across the face of the waters to hasten their evaporation: "God made a wind to pass over the earth, and the waters |subsided|" (Gen. 8:1). Second, He reversed His previous and mysterious subterranean work by which He had released the waters of the earth's interior. Suddenly, the earth closed its gushing fountains: "The fountains also of the deep...were stopped" (v. 2). Third, He opened new crevasses, caverns and fissures to drink in the floodwaters that they might return to the earth's vast interior: "And the waters returned from off the earth continually" (v. 3). Fourth, He broke up the cloud cover and quenched the rains of heaven: "And the rain from heaven was restrained" (v. 2). After the clouds dissipated, blue skies prevailed for seven months, enabling the sun's heat to further hasten the evaporation of the waters: "The waters were abated" (v. 3). Fifth,

God's hand gently guided the rudderless ark to its final berth in the mountains of Ararat, the first firm footing it had known in five months: "And the ark rested…upon the mountains of Ararat" (v. 4). By these tangible interventions God confirmed His presence and help to Noah. The sight of each one of them must have reminded Noah of that greatest of spiritual truths, "God is faithful" (1 Cor. 10:13). Indeed, God had been faithful to him throughout the whole ordeal, watching over, standing by and upholding him. Now, finally, Noah's watery trial had reached a turning point. Never again would his eyes behold the rising waters of death; divine deliverance was underway. To these acts God added a series of special signs.

His signs

Two and a half months after the ark settled down on presumably the highest peak in the Ararat range, Noah sighted other mountaintops rising out of the waters: "The tops of the mountains [were] seen" (Gen. 8:5). Forty days later, he began sending out a dove weekly to determine the proximity of his release. At first, the dove returned with no evidence of life (v. 9); this told Noah that not even the treetops were visible yet. A week later the dove returned with "an olive leaf plucked off" (v. 11); by this he understood that some treetops were now exposed. After another week, the dove didn't return at all (v. 12); thus Noah knew that somewhere in the nearby mountains or lowlands the dove had found dry ground upon which to land. A month later Noah sighted dry ground in the valleys below him: "Noah removed the covering of the ark, and looked, and behold, the face [surface only] of the ground was dry" (v. 13). This long-awaited sight undoubtedly filled Noah with an overwhelmingly joyful sense of anticipation. He now knew that each passing day brought him nearer to a reborn earth, a new life and a better world. Hence, his hope and his joy grew stronger by the hour. To these divine signs God added His Word.

His Word

Fifty-seven days after Noah sighted dry ground, the earth was fully dried and ready for use. (See Genesis 8:14.) So, to signal that the time for debarkation had come, God spoke: "And God spoke unto Noah, saying, Go forth from the ark" (vv. 15–16). Aside from its historical significance—God was re-creating the human race by His word (compare Genesis 1:3–27)—this heavenly *logos* was a tremendous personal relief to Noah, for he had not heard a word from God in an entire year. Since uttering the memorable command, "Come thou and all thy house into the ark" (Gen. 7:1), God had been silent. It had been a long, demanding trial of faith and endurance, but now, twelve months later, it was over. So Noah's test ended as it had begun—with a word from God.

～

Thus by speaking again, granting signs and renewing His actions, God fully "remembered" His seemingly forgotten servant.

DO YOU *FEEL* FORGOTTEN?

Have you been confined to a very long trial of faith, as Noah was? Does it seem as if the Lord who constrained and led you into your "ark," or troubled circumstances, has since lost sight of you in the large and churning sea of humanity? Having been long without His words, signs and acts, do you now *feel* (though you know better) as if He has forgotten you?

Then remember Noah's five months of intense, sustained adversity, during which his situation became more hopeless by the day. And remember his larger, concurrent trial—his full year of silence—during which God required him to walk by faith in His initial word of promise and gave encouraging signs only as he neared its end. Also, understand that God is not terminating you; He's testing you. He's trusting you, as He did Noah, to keep your trust in Him when every visible, worldly fact mocks your faith and shouts that God has forgotten you. So believe God—that at His appointed time of intervention, the God of Noah will faithfully remember you and begin turning your deluge into delight. Suddenly, and thereafter steadily, everything that has been against you will be miraculously turned in your favor.

Your torrents of adversity will finally cease, the Son of Righteousness will break through and shine upon you with favor, and a warm breeze of hope will begin blowing through your soul. New sources of help will open and swallow the swelling troubles that have been rising steadily against you. Your seemingly endless stream of difficulties will stop, and a new river, a joyous flow of fulfillments, will break out. Your previously unstable circumstances will settle down as the Spirit of God leads you to your personal Ararat, or divinely appointed resting place. Then signs will appear. You will see visible indications, divine hints, that plainly tell you the full end of your demanding test is at hand. And finally, God's word of release will come to you. The Spirit will bring a scripture to mind, effectively commanding you to "go forth" and begin your new season of fulfillment. Then you will realize with new conviction that you must henceforth walk by faith, not feeling. The facts of God's presence, power and promises (see chapter 14, page 135) are as unchangeable as He is: "For I am the LORD; I change not" (Mal. 3:6; see Hebrews 13:8). These great pillars of Christian life never vary, regardless of outward appearances or our innermost feelings. And you will also grasp with a stronger conviction the great truth Noah realized the day he again set foot on dry ground: God is faithful after all! You will know that you know that He has been faithful to you! He didn't forget you; He can't forget you; He will never forget you. Or as Jesus assured us in His unchanging Word, "I will never leave thee, nor forsake thee" (Heb. 13:5).

Truly, as God is not a man that He should lie, so He is not a man that He should forget. Hence, Isaiah bids us never moan that God has forgotten us:

> Why sayest thou, O Jacob, and speakest, O Israel, My way is hidden from the LORD, and Ithe justice due to me is passed awayl from my God?
>
> —ISAIAH 40:27

> But Zion said, The LORD hath forsaken me, and my LORD hath forgotten me. Can a woman forget her Inursingl child, that she should not have compassion on the son of her womb? Yea, they may forget, *yet will I not forget thee.*
>
> —ISAIAH 49:14–15, EMPHASIS ADDED

With Noah's example before you, don't allow the "moan" to rest in your heart. If you do, even though you are rightly related to God and unquestionably closer to Him than your enemies, you will find the Spirit dealing with you to repent.

Chapter Sixteen

WHEN THE RIGHTEOUS REPENT

Judgment must begin at the house of God...*at us.*
—1 PETER 4:17, EMPHASIS ADDED

Considerable biblical evidence establishes the following spiritual principle:

IN TIMES OF VISITATION, GOD

CORRECTS THE BEST FIRST.

Surprisingly, His rod strikes not those headed for judgment but those destined for glory. Emphatically, the God of the righteous insists that His own fully obey His will before He punishes the unrighteous for their more obvious rebellion.

At such times, a self-righteous attitude will hinder us from receiving God's visitation. As long as we refuse to deal with our remaining sins, God refuses to intervene in our troubles. But when we humble ourselves by confessing our sinful attitudes and actions and putting them away, He visits and blesses us with deliverances and fulfillments. Consider the following cases in the inspired records of the court of holy writ.

THE CASE OF JOB

Most of the dialogue in the Book of Job chronicles the lengthy and often caustic dispute between Job and his three friends-turned-enemies, as well as a final speech made by Elihu, a young man who felt inspired to rebuke both Job and his argumentative critics. (See Job 3–31; 32–37.) At long last, the time came for the Judge of all the earth to set things straight.

Yet when God finally moved in judgment, in an incredible twist, He dealt *first* with Job, whom He had repeatedly (and infallibly) described as His "perfect and upright" servant. (See Job 1:1, 8; 2:3.) Startlingly, from heaven's bench, its Judge rebuked Job soundly and sternly. (See Job 38–41.) His reprimand came not for any secret sins, such as his friends had suspected, but for the sinful attitude Job had developed over the course of his long and baffling trial, namely, the pride and strife of self-vindication.

When Job's life suddenly fell apart due to a series of apparently obvious divine judgments (Job 1–2), his friends initially comforted him with pure mercy and precious silent support (Job 2:11–13). But after seven days, their religious pride stood up to condemn the man they assumed God had judged. In a display of amazing callousness, they heaped countless false accusations of secret sin on Job's wounded heart, suffering body and shocked and confused mind. Given Job's extreme condition, the cold audacity of his formerly warm friends was more than he was willing to take. In short

156

order, an epic argument ignited. By standing up to decry his unjust prosecution, Job sought to vindicate himself and thus regain his friends' respect by force of words. In attempting to do so, he lost his two greatest virtues, humility and patience, and gave place to an uplifting spirit of self-righteousness (religious pride). According to the Bible's unmistakable and unmistaken testimony (Job 1:22; 2:10), Job committed no sin whatsoever until he opened his mouth to complain and vindicate himself before his disloyal friends. Their sin was their reaction to his plight—assuming the worst and making firm judgments without evidence—for which God later rebuked them. And Job's sin was his reaction to their reaction, for which God also, and first, rebuked him.

God's overpowering tongue-lashing of Job did not stop until Job was truly broken and ashamed of his attitude. Though he had defended himself vigorously before his three friends, Job eventually humbled himself before the Lord. When the Convicter's word-arrows finally pierced Job's thick, self-righteous armor, the thought hit him: His proud, self-defensive words were themselves sin. Immediately, he ceased his self-justifying tirade:

> Then Job answered the LORD, and said, Behold, I am vile; what shall I answer thee? I will lay mine hand upon mine mouth. Once have I spoken, but I will not answer [any more]; yea, twice, but I will proceed no further [in heated self-defense].
>
> —JOB 40:3–5

A short while later, thoroughly humbled by the searing blast of God's mouth, Job uttered words of unconditional surrender: "I abhor myself, and repent in dust and ashes" (Job 42:6). That was all God was waiting to hear.

Job's confession set in motion a glorious visitation of God. The moment Job ended his words of humble repentance

157

God began His work of righteous judgment and restoration. First, He moved quickly to rebuke Job's accusers, making clear to them that Job, whom He referred to four times as "my servant," had been right with Him all along: "My wrath is kindled against thee…for ye have not spoken of me the thing that is right, *as my servant Job hath*" (vv. 7–8, emphasis added). Second, He ordered them to seek prayer-help from Job, as proof of the sincerity of their repentance: "Go to my servant, Job…and my servant, Job, shall pray for you" (v. 8). Third, the narrative also implies He asked Job (directly, or indirectly through their request) to pray for his persecutors in order to prove the sincerity of his humility and mercy. (See verse 10.) Fourth, He ended Job's horrible captivity, reversing all the shocking adversities He had permitted to test Job's faith and loyalty. When Job prayed for his enemies, suddenly he was healed, restored, vindicated and lovingly reunited with all his family members and former friends: "And the LORD turned the captivity of Job, when he prayed for his friends…Then came there unto him all his brethren, and all his sisters, and all they that had been of his acquaintance before, and did eat bread with him in his house" (vv. 10–11). And as a special token of His delight in Job's attitude of total surrender, God gave Job a double portion of everything he had lost: "Also the LORD gave Job twice as much as he had before" (42:10). So the Lord visited and blessed His righteous servant Job.

But note the spiritual hinge upon which Job's captivity turned: *God did not intervene until Job, not his accusers, repented. It was his change of attitude that precipitated the great wave of blessing.* Though the biblical record clearly states that Job was God's best man—"there is none like him in the earth" (Job 1:8; 2:3)—God required him to humble himself first.

THE CASE OF MOSES

When it was time for the Israelites' release from Egyptian

bondage, God sent Moses to deliver his brethren. But before Moses could deliver his brethren, he had to be delivered—not from idolatry or gross wickedness, but from one isolated point of disobedience.

Though he knew God had commanded all Hebrew males to be circumcised, Moses failed to circumcise his second son, Eliezer, during his latter years in Midian. Graciously, God endured patiently with Moses, hoping he would correct the problem voluntarily. But, ungraciously, Moses didn't respond. So, with the Exodus at hand, God was forced to bring Moses to judgment. The Just One visited Moses "by the way in the inn" (Exod. 4:24), causing him to become deathly ill. Strange as it sounds to our soft Laodicean ears, God then gave His handpicked, long-trained servant a very sobering choice: Do or die. That is, do what I say now or pay with your life! Why was God so stern? The reason is simple. It was time for His judgment to begin, and, as always, His way was to reckon with His own first. Hence, He demanded that Moses repent of his private sin before He sent him to demand repentance of Pharaoh for his gross public sin—the horrible oppression of the Israelites.

Or, from a different perspective, God plagued Moses first. The sickness that befell Moses on his return to Egypt was every bit a divine plague, exactly the type and severity of heavenly pressure that later befell Pharaoh and his people for their cruel sins. And it came for the same reason—to induce an attitude of repentance toward God and full compliance with His will. Moreover, it was equally effective; during his illness Moses repented and complied with the divine will by having Zipporah belatedly circumcise Eliezer. (See Exodus 4:25.) Not until this point did God release Moses to return to Egypt and release His judgments on the ungodly Egyptians: "So he let him go" (v. 26). After Moses' arrival in Egypt, he witnessed God's plagues striking Pharaoh and his people just as they had smitten him earlier, albeit with an ultimately different result.

So in the case of Moses, once more, the repentance of the righteous induced the visitation of God. *Moses' repentance, not Pharaoh's, sent him on his way to speedily deliver his long-oppressed brethren.*

THE CASE OF DAVID

For over a decade King Saul's cruel and unjustified persecution of David angered God. Yet before divine judgment fell on Israel's apostate leader, it fell first on his righteous replacement, David. Why was this necessary?

Sixteen months earlier, David's faith had suffered a serious lapse. After years of being chased from one end of Israel to the other by Saul's men, David flagged in his endurance and his previously firm confidence in God's faithfulness. The Bible reveals the tiny but powerful thought that turned David's heart and his entire life from the faith: "And David said in his heart, I shall now perish one day by the hand of Saul; there is nothing better for me than that I should speedily escape into the land of the Philistines" (1 Sam. 27:1). Once David accepted this lie (that Saul would eventually kill him if he remained in Israel) and its accompanying "good idea" (to flee for his life), his faith failed. He then promptly forsook his place of blessing (Israel), sought refuge in Philistia and eventually settled in the city of Ziklag. (See 1 Samuel 27:2–7.)

Now fear, not faith, had ordered David's hasty relocation. Hence, by obeying the voice of unbelief, David had departed from God's will—and His protection. Ziklag was enemy territory. The everlasting wings hovered over Israel, but not Philistia. Once established there, David became a soul profoundly out of place: God's man living on the devil's ground. For this disbelieving departure from God's will and David's sixteen-month-long failure to correct himself, divine chastening was necessary.

So, faithfully and wisely, the heavenly Father gave His

erring son what he needed—a circumstantial spanking! He permitted the Amalekites to sweep through Ziklag, burn the city, and kidnap its residents, including David's wives and children. (See 1 Samuel 30:1–5.) Though from a human perspective the Amalekites' cruel raid was Satan's attempt to utterly destroy David's faith and family just before he received his long-awaited kingship, from heaven's viewpoint it was God's hand urging David to leave the land of unbelief and return to the land of faith. Undeniably, the crisis forced him to look again in faith to the Lord. When "greatly distressed" over his missing wives and children, David realized one thing: It was time to seek the Lord. So "David encouraged himself in the LORD his God…and David inquired of the LORD" (1 Sam. 30:6–8). After being long in unbelief, this earnest turning to God for help was an act of repentance; he who had fallen by doubting was again putting his trust in the Lord. Though it is not stated, David's actions at Ziklag (and his subsequent writings; see Psalm 32:5, 10) indicate that he confessed his sins of unbelief and self-led living and asked God for forgiveness before he asked for help in the crisis. Then, only days after David recovered all, God intervened by judging Saul (1 Sam. 31:1–6) and bringing David to the throne of Judah (2 Sam. 2:1–4). Thus He delivered David and every other Israelite from Saul's ungodly leadership.

God's pattern of action here is unmistakable: *He reckoned with David, who was clearly the "better" man (1 Sam. 15:28), and David responded in repentance; then God reckoned with David's cruel adversary.* Hence, yet again, He judged the righteous before the unrighteous.

BIBLICALLY UNMISTAKABLE YET WIDELY UNKNOWN

Isaiah asserts that God's thinking is infinitely higher and often altogether different than ours:

For my thoughts are not your thoughts, neither are your

ways my ways, saith the LORD. For as the heavens are
higher than the earth, so are my ways higher than your
ways, and my thoughts than your thoughts.

—ISAIAH 55:8–9

This is certainly evident in the matter before us in this
chapter. If God had consulted us concerning the cases of Job,
Moses and David, we would have advised Him to reverse His
dealings. From our viewpoint, Job's judgmental friends
should have been taken to task before Job was rebuked; they
were far guiltier than he. And we would surely have plagued
Pharaoh first, not Moses, who was "very meek, above all the
men who were upon the face of the earth" (Num. 12:3);
tyrants should be punished before saints. Furthermore, we
would never have humiliated David at Ziklag, since from a
human perspective Saul's relentless, demonic pursuit pres-
sured David into his flight to Philistia; Saul should have
received major judgment before David received minor correction. Or so we think. Why do we feel this way?

At least two reasons are apparent. First, as stated above,
many Christians simply haven't studied Scripture enough to
know God's thoughts or His ways as they are repeatedly
revealed therein. Second, we usually prefer to compare ourselves with others rather than humbly correct ourselves by the
plain, righteous standards of God's Word. We see others'
faults, presume theirs are worse than ours, and conclude
smugly that therefore God will surely accept us as we are. Our
antagonists need to repent, but not us; God's wrath is surely on
them, but not on us. Human pride always insists that its adversaries get right *now*, while it calmly ignores its own faults. But
in Scripture and in life the Holy Spirit consistently reverses
this order. In the Sermon on the Mount, Jesus taught us
explicitly to concentrate on correcting our sins and shortcom-
ings first, not those of our fellow Christians and antagonists:
"Thou hypocrite, *first* cast the beam out of thine own eye, and

162

then shalt thou see clearly to cast the mote out of thy brother's eye" (Matt. 7:5, emphasis added). Why did He teach this? Because it is His Father's way. Whenever He intervenes in the affairs of this world to judge and bless, the heavenly Father always chastens His children first. We suffer His rod before His (and our) enemies suffer His sword. He pressures us to be pure before He punishes them for persecuting us. This principle of the repentance of the righteous appears throughout the Bible. It is even present in the End-Time prophecies.

As sustained, extensive teaching of God's Word goes forth through divinely chosen ministers in these last days, the Holy Spirit will systematically "judge" Christ's true followers worldwide; that is, He will identify for removal every spot, wrinkle and blemish in our spiritual characters. (See Ephesians 5:26–27.) This divinely inspired Christian sanctification movement—the start of God's worldwide process of judgment (see 1 Peter 4:17)—will begin unfolding soon. By the outpouring of God's power, the enlightenment of His Word, the conviction of His Spirit and, as needed, the heavenly Father's corrective counsel through pastors and His chastening through adverse circumstances, the wise will gradually learn to judge their sin and carnality and walk closely with Jesus in healthy self-examination and true holiness. As this spiritual growth continues, fiery trials will come to test the mettle of God's uncompromising ones, but they will only further the cleansing and strengthening process of His vessels unto honor. Tare-Christians, those who consistently refuse to be made holy, will be removed from among God's overcomers by divinely induced separations and other kinds of divine judgments. (See Matthew 13:30, 40–43.) Thus, while still in this present world, the true church (body of righteous ones worldwide) will be deeply cleansed and made ready for her Lord. Or, as stated above, it will be "judged"—restored to divine order by steady, unyielding divine pressure.

163

Sometime after this judgment of the righteous has run its course, at God's appointed time, Jesus will appear (1 Thess. 4:16–17), receive His overcoming church (John 14:3) and "present" her to Himself (Eph. 5:27) in glorious heavenly union. For the next seven years, God's worldwide judgment process will run its course among the unrighteous. At its end, the Lord will return to earth and smite the blasphemous beast and his sin-hardened followers, who will have cruelly persecuted Christ's followers both before and during the Tribulation drama. So the day of vengeance will close with God's judgment of the unrighteous.

Even in these last days, therefore, the Lord will purge unholiness from the redeemed before He pours wrath on the unredeemed. The apostle Peter observed, "And if it [divine judgment] first begin at us, what shall the end be of them that obey not the gospel of God?" (1 Pet. 4:17). So as it was in the beginning, so it will be in the end: The righteous will be reckoned with first.

DO YOU NEED GOD'S HELP?

Do you need God's help in your present circumstances? Are you, like Job, enduring the painful final stages of a long-lasting standoff with judgmental former friends? Are you, like David, waiting for God to bring you to a place of ministry to which you have long felt called? Are you, like Moses, hoping the Lord will use you to help deliver your spiritual brothers and sisters from the oppression of the devil? Then think it not strange if God's Spirit bears down on your conscience first, before He subdues your adversaries. Always, His judgments begin "at the house of God" (1 Pet. 4:17); that is, with His own people and especially those closest to Him.

He brought Hannah to the point of surrender first, not Peninnah. (See 1 Samuel 1.) He chastened Jacob first, not Esau. (See Genesis 32–33.) He tested, and so reckoned with

164

Joseph first, before He tested Joseph's wayward brothers. (See Genesis 39–40, 42–45.) He purged the Jerusalem church first, removing its willful sinners (Acts 5:1–11) before He reckoned with its Jewish persecutors, such as Saul of Tarsus (Acts 9:1–9) and King Herod Agrippa I (Acts 12:20–23). So if the Holy Spirit has halted you by the way in the inn and pointed out your remaining sin, don't be surprised. And more importantly, don't defend yourself.

Don't Defend Yourself

Job recited his previous good works—and they were many (Job 29:12–17)—as justification for his present bad attitude, yet God still held him responsible for holding to his proud, striving spirit. Don't repeat his error.

That is, when the Converter presses in, don't recite to Him all your good works, past and present, as a subtle excuse for allowing any sinful thing to remain in your life. "But, Lord, I don't do this, that and the other. I participate in ministry projects and support righteous causes. I help the disadvantaged, the elderly and the poor. I attend my church faithfully, give my tithes and offerings, pray and read my Bible daily." All these things may be true, but none are the object of the Holy Spirit's quiet but unceasing protest in your heart. Remember, He is *holy*; as a patient, persistent perfectionist, He will not rest until you are entirely sanctified. The apostle Paul's inspired prayer for the Thessalonians and for us all is, "And the very God of peace sanctify you *wholly*; and I pray God your *whole* spirit and soul and body be preserved blameless unto the coming of our Lord Jesus Christ" (1 Thess. 5:23, emphasis added). This prayer is ever-present in the mind of the Holy Spirit.

So, always bear in mind that no matter what your pluses, the Holy Spirit will require your minuses. His uncompromising holiness demands that He ask you to surrender everything, including the sin you don't want to give up because you think it is too small to matter.

No Sin Is Small to the Holy Spirit

We must learn the lesson Moses learned by the way in the inn. Put simply, it is that the spirit of rebellion is a big deal to God no matter how small its visible manifestation. Oswald Chambers wrote:

> Never discard a conviction. If it is important enough for the Spirit of God to have brought it to your mind, it is that thing He is detecting. You were looking for a great thing to give up. God is telling you of some tiny thing; but at the back of it there lies the central citadel of obstinacy: I will not give up my right to myself—the thing God intends you to give up if ever you are going to be a disciple of Jesus Christ.[1]

It was Moses' "central citadel of obstinacy" that God assaulted by the way in the inn. As stated earlier, Moses was fully trained in right living and spiritually mature in his thinking and attitudes. His walk with God was perfect (complete), except in one area—circumcision—which, from a human perspective, we may consider small. But after Moses emerged from the Holy Spirit's death-hold, only one thought loomed in his mind: To the Holy Spirit, no sin is small. No matter how insignificant it may appear to us, any disobedience to God's will is inspired by, and gives further place to, the spirit of rebellion against God. The presence of this satanic spirit, which is the very spirit of Antichrist, makes any act of sin a very serious matter to God. He knows that if that little fault remains, it will soon grow into a much bigger one and eventually destroy our entire usefulness to Him. The apostle Paul revealed this in his writings to the Corinthians: "Know ye not that a little leaven leaveneth the whole lump?" (1 Cor. 5:6). Then he wisely urged them and us to put away every sin, including the ones we consider small: "Purge out, therefore, the old leaven, that ye may be a new lump" (v. 7). Are we heeding his advice?

Forget, Focus and Surrender

For the moment, forget the seriousness of your adversaries' sins against God and against you, His servant. If the Lord wills that they tarry till He comes, what is that to you? Focus your full attention instead on the chastening of the Lord in your life. Understand and fully accept that it is you, not your antagonists, whom He seeks to thoroughly purge. John the Baptist declared this—the thorough purging of the saints—to be the primary reason Jesus baptizes Christians with the Holy Spirit: "[The Lord's] fan is in his hand, and he will |*thoroughly*| *purge* his floor" (Matt. 3:12, emphasis added). Why? That, once we are thoroughly sanctified, He may bring us to the place of fulfillment He has prepared for us.

To reach the honorable heights of fulfillment we must pass through the humbling valley of chastisement. Always, "before honor is humility" (Prov. 18:12). As seen repeatedly in this chapter, the heavenly Father corrects the best first. So surrender to Him. Wherever you have previously rebelled against Him, submit. Whatever He says unto you, do it. Endure God's stern rebukes from the "whirlwind" (Job 38:1) and put away your self-pity and your prideful lust for self-vindication. Accept your Ziklag, the destruction of your self-led works. Submit to your Gilgal, God's sudden, strong insistence that you stop loving the things of the world. Cut off all the flesh that hinders you and be fully circumcised in spirit.

But Don't Misunderstand the Just One

In coming to an understanding of this principle, don't misunderstand the actions of the Just One. That He chastens us first does *not* imply He will forever overlook our enemies. As stated above, after judgment begins at God's house, it continues elsewhere. Jesus Himself assured us, "I tell you that he [God] will avenge them [His oppressed children] speedily" (Luke 18:8). How could a just God do otherwise, that is, fail to ultimately avenge His own suffering children who cry to Him for justice day and night? Rest assured, O afflicted one; God will have His day with all His enemies, including yours. He had His day of correction with you, didn't He? If He persistently convicted you, He will also persistently reckon with them. If He thoroughly purged you, He will also thoroughly punish them unless they repent.

EXPECT DIVINE INTERVENTION

The psalmist declared, "No good thing will he withhold from them that walk uprightly" (Ps. 84:11). This is another way of saying we reap what we sow; when we sow uprightness, we reap good things from God. Then know this: If you sow personal repentance, you will reap divine intervention. Immediately after you willingly "forget, focus and surrender," the Lord will begin calming the stormy waters of your life. (See chapter 7.)

Your revilers will hear His voice defending you, and they will be ashamed. Your sorrowful captivity will cease, and your joyful double portion will commence. God will remove from your life those who have willfully hindered you, and you will arise to assume your divinely appointed place of service. Your trying season of spiritual training will end, and you will go forth "a vessel unto honor, sanctified, and |fit| for the master's use, and prepared unto every good work" (2 Tim. 2:21), ready to comfort and deliver weary Christians. Thus, in His own time and way, the Lord will intervene in your life and show Himself strong in your behalf.

So search your heart today and forsake your faults. Then, with the psalmist, expect divine intervention—"great things"—from your God:

Then said they among the |nations|, The LORD hath done great things for them. The LORD hath done great things for us, whereof we are glad.

—PSALM 126:2–3

Exactly when, where and how the Lord will intervene is uncertain, but that He will do so is sure. Until then, be still and trust Him to come to you. Do nothing in your own wisdom or strength to extricate yourself from your difficulties.

Chapter Seventeen

TIME TO DO...
NOTHING

Be still, and know that I am God.

—PSALM 46:10

I t has been wisely said, "When you don't know what to do, don't do anything." To aggressive souls who feel compelled to always take the initiative, this truism may seem weak and negative, but it's not. It's positive wisdom.

So positive, in fact, that when obeyed in its proper time it makes the difference between victory and defeat in our trials. To a man, experienced Christian disciples know that there are indeed times when the best, the wisest, the strongest thing we can do is simply *nothing*. Or to put this in the words of the psalmist: "Be still, and know that I am God" (Ps. 46:10). Various translations of this verse help us broaden this thought:

Let be and be still, and know—recognize and understand—that I am God.

—AMP, EMPHASIS ADDED

Cease striving and know that I am God.

—NAS, EMPHASIS ADDED

Stand silent! Know that I am God!

—TLB, EMPHASIS ADDED

Paraphrasing, we may further enlarge this thought as follows:

Don't speak, work, move, rack your brain for ideas or
rush about seeking ideas or assistance from others to
change your troubled situation. Just be still, believe in
the Lord's faithful character and promises, commune
with Him through His Word and ask His help in prayer.
Then quietly go forward with your duties and trust the
Lord to work and send help in the area of your need.

Of such crucial times Isaiah concluded, "Their [God's
children's] strength is to sit still" (Isa. 30:7).

Some years ago, I read a fascinating account of the
rescue of a polar explorer whose actions perfectly illustrate
this vital spiritual truth.

Saved—by the Wisdom to Trust Another Rather Than Try to Save Himself

An ambitious undertaking for even the most ambitious polar
explorers, the Trans-Antarctica Expedition was a thirty-
seven-hundred mile unmechanized trek (using dogsleds)
across the Antarctican continent, from Seal Nunataks, on the
eastern peninsula near the southernmost tip of South
America, to Mirnyy, a base camp maintained by the former
Soviet Union and located in East Antarctica on the shores of
the Indian Ocean. This remarkable seven-month quest,
which lasted from July 27, 1989, to March 3, 1990, was

undertaken by a six-man team of scientists and explorers, each of whom was from a different nation. Beside the predictable difficulties of such a mission—months of bone-numbing sub-zero temperatures, sudden violent snowstorms, lengthy weather delays, treacherous mountains, deadly snow-concealed crevasses and the ever-present problem of resupply—this multinational team of bravehearts also faced several unpredicted near-disasters. One of them, unquestionably the worst, occurred only two days and sixteen miles from the much-anticipated end of their epic journey.

Late on the afternoon of March 1, 1990, while waiting out yet another ferocious snowstorm (over twenty-four hours), the Japanese member of the team, Keizo Funatsu, a dogsled driver, left his tent to feed his sled dogs. Right away he became lost in the prevailing whiteout—blizzard conditions that cause the snow pack beneath, the falling snow on every side and the clouds above to appear as a solid mass of white, leaving the traveler without sight of the horizon and hence disoriented, without any sure sense of direction, distance or depth. Immediately Funatsu realized it was impossible for him to tell which direction led back to the camp. And in this weather, that meant trouble. Very serious trouble.

Though only thirty-two years old, Funatsu was blessed with enough polar experience to recognize the terrible dangers he faced. If he tried to find his way back to his tent and chose the wrong direction, he might easily walk *away* from safety and quickly freeze to death in the lethal sub-zero temperatures, even in his special protective clothing. (The Chinese member of the expedition, Qin Dahe, had told the others how, on another mission, one of his fellow scientists was caught and disoriented in a whiteout and froze to death despite being between two buildings only fifty yards apart!) Or he might stumble into a crevasse or fissure and fall to his death, never to be found. While he didn't know his location

173

physically, situationally Funatsu knew exactly where he stood: His casual afternoon ramble had taken him from the relative comfort of his tent into the gaping jaws of imminent disaster. And they were closing fast.

But miraculously, Funatsu didn't panic in the crisis. Using a small tool he had in hand, he calmly dug a trench in the snow and curled up in it, deliberately allowing the rapidly accumulating snow to cover him. Surprisingly, it was the same way his sled dogs spent their nights—buried in the snow, which, incredibly, helped *protect* them from the far more dangerous cold and winds of the region, which during the expedition had reached inhuman extremes (–50° F and 90 m.p.h. winds). In a matter of seconds he was completely covered, except for one small cavity he kept open for breathing. For the next thirteen hours, the snow held the temperature in his tiny snow trench at an uncomfortable but bearable level. There, in complete stillness and silence, he awaited help. His thinking at this time and his faith (in his teammates) were the keys to his eventual rescue.

Funatsu decided that since he didn't know which way to go, he would go nowhere; that since he didn't know what to do, he would do nothing...but trust his friends. Instead of trying to rescue himself, which would likely have led to his death, he took refuge in the snow and let his companions rescue him. He knew they would soon realize he was lost, and he believed they would promptly begin searching for him. His saving confidence is best expressed in his own words, penned later in his journal:

> I knew my teammates would be looking for me. I believed I would be found; it was just a matter of time. I had to believe that.
>
> —Keizo Funatsu, Trans-Antarctica Expedition

This faith kept hope alive in Funatsu's heart and enabled

him to endure the bitter conditions that tried his physical and mental endurance to the limit. As if scripted by the very Inspirer of the Bible, events developed according to his faith.

When after one and a half hours (6 P.M.) Funatsu still had not returned to his tent, Will Steger, the expedition leader, and his fellow explorers realized that Funatsu was missing and immediately began searching for him. Holding a rope tied at one end to a secured dog sled, they formed a search line (each man keeping the next just within sight) and swept the area surrounding their camp in a circular motion, continuously probing the snowy darkness with flashlights and calling out their lost friend's name. Despite the absence of any life indicators and the presence of the discouragingly unrelenting storm, they persisted into the night. At 10:30, they stopped for much-needed rest.

At 4 A.M. the next morning, they resumed their search. This time their efforts and Funatsu's patient faith paid off. Around 6 A.M., Funatsu heard their cries, arose from his snow trench and announced joyously in his limited English, "I am alive! I am alive!" Elated, his fellow team members then carried him back to the warmth and safety of his tent. Thus their terror and his trial ceased.

It was an uncomfortably close brush with death—thirteen hours curled up in a snow trench during a fierce blizzard packing some of the deadliest temperatures and winds on earth—but in the end, paradoxically, Funatsu was saved by not trying to save himself and by believing that faithful ones would save him.[1]

ARE YOU CAUGHT IN A SPIRITUAL WHITEOUT?

Similarly, there are times when Christians find themselves unexpectedly caught in and greatly tried by spiritual whiteouts. What is a spiritual whiteout?

Out of the blue, with the speed of a polar blizzard and

often when our trials' ends are tantalizingly close, the enemy hits us with a devastating blow—and suddenly we experience spiritual disorientation. For the moment, we lose all sense of spiritual direction. No aspect of God's will is clearly defined, no alternative seems safe, no way is confirmed by the unerring Word or the peaceful witness of the Spirit. Search as we may, we cannot find God's way of escape; every desirable course of action is blocked by paralyzing impossibilities. Then light comes: This is no ordinary trial; it is the kind of powerful, spiritually deadly onslaught that strikes only once or twice in our lifetime.

Another inspired thought dawns: We must not be self-led; any step taken in the flesh may be our last. It may cause us to fall into a spiritual snowdrift—a lengthy delay in God's plan, like the one David caused by impulsively relocating in Ziklag and wasting sixteen precious months of his life (see chapter 19, pages 201-202), or the one Abraham caused by taking Hagar into his home without divine authorization. (See Genesis 16–21.) Or worse, it may cause us to suddenly drop off into a deadly spiritual crevasse—a rebellious turn from God back to our former selfish, sinful lifestyle—never to return. So, aware of these besieging perils, we stand still and pray for wisdom, knowing only one thing: We don't know what to do. As we grope for understanding through prayer, the Holy Spirit, our ever-present Guide and Teacher, faithfully speaks in our hearts, reminding us of the spiritual whiteouts recorded in biblical history. Among them, the cases of Job and Peter stand out.

One day Job was a very godly, very prosperous believer and a loving family man; the next he was utterly bewildered and brokenhearted, stripped of every possession and bereft of all his children. (See Job 1.) One day Peter was busily ministering the words and works of Christ in the power of the Spirit to multitudes of Christians throughout Israel; the next he was abruptly arrested, isolated and confined to Herod's prison with armed guards surrounding him and a death sentence hanging over his head. (See Acts 12:1–4.) In both cases, these whiteout victims chose the same course of action: Rather than try to save themselves, they chose to be still and trust God to save them. From his uncomfortable snow trench, bewildered, abandoned by his friends and near death, Job declared he would do nothing but trust God: "Though he slay me, yet will I trust in him" (Job 13:15). And in his cold prison cell, Peter chose to believe that his fellow Christians, realizing his peril, would gather and pray for his rescue, and that God would send help.

In both instances, God acted in accord with His servants' faith. As they believed, so it was done unto them. After rebuking Job, He opened up a wonderful way of escape for him. (See chapter 16, pages 156–158.) And on the last night before Peter's scheduled execution, while he slept in perfect trust in God's faithfulness to answer prayer, the Lord sent an angel to rescue him. (See Acts 12:5–11.)

Do Nothing...but Stand!

When we are suddenly caught in similarly extreme spiritual crises, we should employ the wisdom of doing nothing; that is, nothing of ourselves, nothing without God, nothing apart from His clear leading and direction, nothing to try to lift ourselves out of our overwhelming problems by mere human ways and means. Instead, we should dig a faith trench and determinedly take refuge in God until He comes to save us: "O God...my soul trusteth in thee. Yea, in the shadow of thy wings will I make my refuge, until these calamities be |passed by|" (Ps. 57:1).

Or, to change the symbol somewhat, we should heed the Living Bible's paraphrase of Psalm 46:10: "*Stand silent!* Know that I am God" (emphasis added). This was also the apostle Paul's wise counsel to Christians who are under attack. A skilled survivor of many spiritual whiteouts, Paul advised: "Having done all, to *stand*" (Eph. 6:13, emphasis added). Spiritually speaking, to stand is to remain unmoved, upright, trusting and silent. In spiritual crises, we stand by:

1. *Not* lashing out in anger to resist injustice or spite
2. *Not* fainting with panic
3. *Not* turning and walking away from the Lord, offended
4. *Not* running ahead of Him anxiously at our own initiative

And by:

1. Maintaining close fellowship with the Lord daily
2. Continuing in our current duties
3. Believing in the Lord's unchanging faithfulness and mercy—that He sees our desperation and will surely save us

Pragmatic Christians will be hard pressed to find a more effective method than this, for the inspired record plainly shows that *it works!* King Jehoshaphat is a case in point.

When Jehoshaphat and all Judah were unexpectedly caught in a spiritual whiteout in 2 Chronicles 20:1–30—suddenly surrounded by a hostile and vastly larger military force—God commanded His people not to fight, but rather to simply be still, fix their hearts in trust and watch Him save them: "Ye shall not need to fight in this battle; set yourselves, stand ye still, and see the salvation of the LORD with you" (v. 17). Wisely, they chose to obey Him. The only thing they did was to "stand"—be still, believe in His faithfulness and praise Him for His unfailing mercy (vv. 20–22). Consequently, the Lord intervened and saved them. Why? Because, obediently, they did *not* try to save themselves in the battle at hand. Theirs is a grand example to follow.

Tempted to Save Yourself?

When the temptation to save yourself—to do anything you can to escape and find relief—presses hard, you must not yield. Rather than kindle fires of self-deliverance, you should quietly warm your heart with the belief that God, your God, your just, compassionate, all-knowing, all-powerful, very present Helper in trouble, will come to your rescue. By doing this, you "stay" yourself upon God:

> Who is among you that feareth the LORD, that obeyeth the voice of his servant, that walketh in darkness, and hath no light? Let him trust in the name of the LORD, and *stay upon his God.*
>
> —ISAIAH 50:10, EMPHASIS ADDED

Thus you enter into the rest of faith. What a glorious relief it is to discover you don't have to find a way out of your dilemma. If you will just hold steady, God will find you. If you will only occupy, He will come to you. Hasn't He promised this in His Word?

> Occupy till I come.
>
> —LUKE 19:13

> I will not leave you comfortless; I will come to you.
>
> —JOHN 14:18

> Be strong, fear not; behold, your God will come...he will come and save you.
>
> —ISAIAH 35:4

Inability is no excuse for noncompliance. If Job, Peter and Jehoshaphat—and even unbelievers, like Keizo Funatsu!—could be still and trust in the height of their crises, so can you. You can do all things through Christ who strengthens you! Doubt is no excuse either. If God came to their rescue, He will come to yours, too; He is no respecter of persons. Neither is ignorance any longer a reason you should fail. You now know what God would have you do when you're hit by powerful spiritual whiteouts. Only one question, then, remains: Will you do it?

If you won't, you can forget walking on water; you'll slip and plummet beneath your troubled waters like a rock. Defeated by trial, your confidence in God and your usefulness to Him will then gradually diminish. But if you will, that is, if you will refuse to wander off into the way-less, hopeless perplexity of your blinding spiritual whiteout, God will do whatever it takes to save you. His all-seeing eyes remain on constant alert, ever searching the world over for trusting souls in need of rescue: "For the eyes of the LORD run to and fro throughout the whole earth, to show himself strong in the behalf of them whose heart is perfect [trusting] toward him" (2 Chron. 16:9). If necessary, He will send a party of "angels," angelic or human, to meet you and lift you out of your distress before it's too late. And thereafter you will trust and serve Him ever more.

In the end, ironically, you will save yourself by not trying to save yourself—because you trust God to do so. And God's help always comes at just the right time.

Chapter Eighteen

Divine Intervention Divinely Timed

God is faithful, who will…make the way to escape.
—1 Corinthians 10:13

Triumphantly, the Scriptures declare that God faithfully makes a way of escape for His faithful ones: "God is faithful, who will not |permit| you to be tempted above that ye are able, but will, with the temptation, also make |the| way to escape, that ye may be able to bear it" (1 Cor. 10:13). But God's help, though sure, is not always swift. He sometimes chooses to "bear long" with us in the midst of our afflictions. (See Luke 18:7.) If He does so, His tarrying is never accidental. He always has good reasons for His delays. Succinctly, two of His chief reasons are:

1. He waits for the moment of faith's greatest development.

2. He waits for the moment of our greatest personal advantage.

Let's examine these points in more detail.

THE MOMENT OF FAITH'S GREATEST DEVELOPMENT

What do we mean by "faith's greatest development"? Simply this: In the trial of faith, the longer we wait for God in the spirit of patient trust, the greater the faith God builds into us. (See chapter 7, pages 70–71.) Typically, Christians feel that the shorter the trial, the better it is, for we all naturally desire deliverance and relief from stressful circumstances *ASAP!* But from the divine perspective, just the opposite is true: The longer the trial, the better the trial. Why? Because as we believe God, obey Him and wait for His help, the difficulty of waiting enlarges our souls. David, whose faith God stretched and strengthened over the course of many long trials, wrote, "Thou hast enlarged me when I was in distress" (Ps. 4:1). Hence, the longer our trials, the more productive they are—the greater the faith, patience and maturity of character they develop in our souls. David was not the only Bible hero whose faith was enlarged by the difficulty of waiting. Consider these others who endured to the moment of faith's greatest development.

The Israelites in Egypt

The Israelites' fiery trial of Egyptian bondage was extremely long. For over four hundred years they languished in "the iron furnace…of Egypt" (Deut. 4:20) as Pharaoh's harried and hopeless slaves. (See Exodus 12:40–42.) When Moses arrived to lead them with miraculous power and heavenly words in tow, they thought surely their long nightmare would soon end. But Jehovah was not finished stretching the faith and endurance of the people whom He hoped to soon give the Promised Land. Disappointingly, Moses' intervention produced yet another period of delay, as Pharaoh's stubbornness caused the long standoff of the plagues. Day after dreary day and week after gloomy week passed without the full deliverance the downtrodden Hebrews so desperately needed. (See Exodus 5–11.) Finally, after the judgment of the Passover night, it seemed evident to all that full liberation was at hand. (See Exodus 12.) And for the next three days, their dream-come-true deliverance lived and spoke and breathed life into their formerly listless spirits. But, incredibly, God still wasn't finished stretching their faith.

Ostensibly, His reason for elongating their trial further was simple enough: Pharaoh still wasn't finished resisting Him. So, with their backs literally to the Red Sea, the Israelites made their final stand against their relentless oppressor. (See Exodus 14.) This final episode in their long trial was itself a seemingly interminable ordeal, for the Lord required the Israelites to tarry "all that night" (v. 21), while both final deliverance and ultimate catastrophe hung precariously in the balances. Even as they walked, hopped and trotted hurriedly down their divinely opened way of escape, a dry sea bed bordered by two imposing walls of water, their victory was not assured, for the Egyptians were still in full pursuit. Then, just before dawn, in the final hour of the morning watch, God sent the waters crashing down on their pursuers. (See Exodus 14:1–31.) Characteristically, it was a last-moment deliverance; if Jehovah had waited any longer, the Egyptians would have overtaken and decimated Israel's traumatized and weary citizen army.

Thus, the Israelites' long "evil day" of Egyptian bondage ended, thanks to God's perfectly timed assistance. And their faith—certainly Moses'—was enlarged as much as possible for the present.

Peter in Herod's prison

"Now about that time Herod, the king, stretched forth his hands to vex certain of the church" (Acts 12:1). And about that time Jesus, the Author and Perfecter of faith, undertook to enlarge the faith of His young church by permitting two huge waves of persecution to suddenly arise and buffet their formerly calm ecclesiastical ship.

First, as the Passover season drew near, King Herod's men arrested the apostle James and executed him (v. 2). Second, just before the Passover feast, Herod struck again, this time arresting and detaining the apostle Peter. Herod planned to execute Peter as he had James as soon as the Passover week (Feast of Unleavened Bread) ended (vv. 3–4). Both Peter's faith and that of the entire church were tested by the sudden, unjust execution of one apostle and the imminent execution of another—its most indispensable leader and preacher of the gospel.

For eight long days the painful waiting game was played out. Herod held Peter in his firmest grip, detaining him in his inner prison and assigning round-the-clock protection by four guard teams of four men each. (Herod was well aware of Peter's previous supernatural escape; see Acts 5:17–25.) Meanwhile, the Christians kept Peter in their most fervent prayer focus, gathering at Mary's house for round-the-clock intercession for his release (Acts 12:5). Yet, despite their faithful fervor, no immediate changes were forthcoming. Day after day, the prayer watchers' report was discouragingly the same: Peter was still in jail, his armed guards were still present, and his execution day was still drawing closer. Finally, on the last night before Peter's scheduled execution, the saints' prayers prevailed and God acted, sending an angel to facilitate Peter's escape (vv. 6–19).

It was another late-hour intervention, coming just before the dawn of Peter's "E-day."

Abraham on Mount Moriah

Beset behind and before by two conflicting words from God—a promise to bless Isaac and a command to kill him—Abraham nevertheless went onward in simple obedience to his most recent orders from on high. (See Genesis 22.) For three excruciatingly long days the patriarch journeyed toward Mount Moriah (vv. 3–4), his heavy heart trusting that God would raise Isaac from death, if necessary, to fulfill His initial promise to bless him. (See Hebrews 11:17–19.) Believing God could do such a miracle, yet not knowing how He would, Abraham's faith was stretched to its spiritual limit. Loving his son, yet loving God even more, Abraham's soul was also exercised to its emotional limit. As day one of this painful test became day two, and then day three, the spiritual pressure mounted. The third day, the minutes must have passed like hours and the hours like weeks.

On that climactic day, Abraham proved his trust in God to the limit. In the calm strength of a heart fixed in trust, he finished his journey, confessed his faith to Isaac, built an altar, set the wood in order, bound Isaac, placed him on the altar and, grasping his knife, raised his hand to finish the ultimate sacrifice. (See Genesis 22:4–10.) Just then, when his hand was raised to strike, God intervened, calling Abraham to stop immediately: "Abraham, Abraham...lay not thine hand upon the lad, neither do thou anything unto him" (vv. 11–12). Then He provided a way of escape by calling Abraham's attention to a fitting substitute for Isaac, "a ram caught in a thicket by his horns" (v. 13).

David's wilderness trials

Throughout his decade of wilderness trials, David lived under the constant threat of attack from Saul. This perpetual harassment often rendered David physically exhausted and emotionally drained. At one point, the lengthy conflict came to a head. (See 1 Samuel 23:25–29.)

In what looked certain to be David's final—and fatal—test, King Saul and his men "compassed David and his men round about to take them" (v. 26). But just before David's faith broke, God broke in—not directly, but providentially. Just when Saul was poised to eliminate David, he received word that a Philistine invasion was underway: "There came a messenger unto Saul, saying, Haste thee, and come; for the Philistines have invaded the land" (v. 27). Immediately Saul was forced to withdraw, leaving David safe and free. Two vital truths prompted this timely divine intervention.

First, David had to be helped immediately. If God had waited any longer, Saul and death would have overtaken Jesse's anointed son. Second, nothing short of a full-scale Philistine invasion (an imminent threat to national security) would have forced Saul to break off his demonically driven manhunt. So, to save His anointed, God did what had to be done when it had to be done. The result was divine deliverance divinely timed.

~

In each of the cases above, God stood by, monitoring the pressure of the trial. He deliberately let the spiritual tension build and build and build—until His servants' faith and patience, and sometimes their psychological and physical endurance, had been exercised to the limit. Then He intervened and stopped the adversity. Invariably, such experiences developed His servants' faith. They trusted Him more for having gone through these crises and having witnessed firsthand His marvelous and faithful deliverance. But the attentive student of Scripture will note this key fact: The Lord did not stop their "stretching process" prematurely. Why? Because if He had, His servants' faith could not have been developed to the maximum. As a result, they would have remained relatively weak, immature and underdeveloped, and hence unfit for the roles He predestined them to play and the tasks He wanted them to accomplish in His wise master-plan for the ages.

THE MOMENT OF OUR GREATEST PERSONAL ADVANTAGE

Romans 8:28 lays down one of the largest foundational facts that support every true Christian's house of faith:

> And we know that God causes all things to work together for good to those who love God, to those who are called according to His purpose.
>
> —ROMANS 8:28, NAS

The wearisome and occasionally overwhelming stresses of our trials of faith tend to make us forget this wonderful Word-pillar. Nevertheless, it remains true that while we continue to obey His Word and follow His call amid our trials, God personally causes all the events, changes and conditions that touch our lives, whether near or far, to work together for our eventual blessing. In His all-powerful goodwill, He turns even the most adverse events—beginning, controlling, turning, ending and thus using them—into forces that ultimately work to our advantage. (See chapter 2, pages 21–23.)

The "moment of our greatest personal advantage" is that time when God's working of all things together for our good has run its course and culminates in an overwhelmingly joyful visitation of divinely coordinated blessings. Suddenly, and often when we least expect it, the Worker of all Things unveils all the blessings He has been personally planning and carefully preparing for us for many years. Observe how He did so for His servants.

Mordecai

"On that night" in which Haman arose to kill Mordecai, God arose—inducing history's most famous case of royal insomnia—to put an end to Haman: "*On that night* could not the king sleep" (Esther 6:1, emphasis added). Restless, King Ahasuerus got up and commanded a late-night reading of his

187

chronicles, during which he was freshly reminded that Mordecai had saved his life and was long overdue for honor. Meanwhile God used Haman's wife to suggest that he should go to the palace that very night to seek the king's permission to put Mordecai to death. In the almost comical sequence of events that followed, Haman was forced to personally lead the citywide parade that was held in Shushan to honor Mordecai (vv. 4–14). A sweeter vindication could not have been imagined for Mordecai, who had suffered the bitterest kind of hatred and persecution from his Amalekite foe. Then on the very next day, Haman's life took an even worse turn. Inspired by Mordecai's public acclamation, Esther boldly exposed Haman's malicious plot to destroy her people. King Ahasuerus, understandably angered by Haman's abuse of royal power, immediately executed him. (See Esther 7:1–10.)

After Haman's death, Esther personally introduced Mordecai to the king and informed him that Mordecai had been her guardian. (See Esther 8:1.) Having been so recently impressed with Mordecai's outstanding integrity, faithfulness and courage, the king recognized that Mordecai would be an excellent choice to replace Haman as prime minister of Persia. So he immediately appointed him to the post: "And the king took off his ring, which he had taken from Haman, and gave it unto Mordecai" (v. 2). What a turnabout! Haman, the evil royal administrator, falls in a public, shameful execution, while Mordecai, his maligned-but-righteous enemy, rises to assume his high office: "For Mordecai, the Jew, was next unto King Ahasuerus, and great among the Jews" (Esther 10:3). At no other time could Mordecai have received such a meteoric rise to power. Only in that hour of special vindication, prompted by Haman's very public incrimination and judgment, did God grant such a high degree of favor to His people in Persia—Esther, Mordecai and all the Jews.

But note this: God deliberately withheld His intervention

until "that night" (Esther 6:1). Why? Because right up to that moment He was extraordinarily busy working all things—Vashti's deposing, Esther's selection as queen, Mordecai's trial of faith, the Jews' trial of slander and persecution, Esther's trial of courage, the fullness of Haman's sin, the final arrogance and delusion of his pride, King Ahasuerus' long failure to honor Mordecai and his apparently ordinary case of insomnia that caused Haman's plot to suddenly unravel—together for their good. Nevertheless, when the moment of Mordecai's greatest personal advantage came, God acted without delay. And suddenly Mordecai saw all the previously hidden blessings God had been preparing for him—deliverance, justice, honor, favor, promotion, wealth and a wide ministry to His people. (See Esther 8:3–10:3.)

The Shunammite

The Shunammite woman, whose son Elisha raised from death, obeyed the prophet's call to sojourn in Philistia during a seven-year famine. (See 2 Kings 8:1–6.) "At the seven year's end," she returned and asked the king of Israel for permission to reclaim her possessions. Little did she know it, but the moment of her greatest personal advantage had arrived.

The very minute she and her son entered the king's court, Elisha's servant Gehazi was describing her son's miracle to the king:

> As he [Gehazi] was telling the king how he had restored a dead body to life…behold, the woman, whose son he had restored to life, |appealed| to the king for her house and for her land. And Gehazi said, My lord, O king, this is the woman, and this is her son, whom Elisha restored to life.
> —2 KINGS 8:5, EMPHASIS ADDED

Delighted to meet the woman God had favored with such a great miracle, the king decided that he too should show her great favor. So he promptly appointed a royal officer to restore her house and land and to ensure that she be paid any profits her farm had produced during her absence: "Restore all that was hers, and all the fruits of the field since the day that she left the land, even until now" (v. 6).

Thus God ended her trial, and she appealed for restitution, at the perfect time. At no other time would she have received such generous treatment.

Joseph

After Joseph interpreted the dream of Pharaoh's butler, it seems clear that he hoped the butler would win him a speedy pardon from Pharaoh. (See Genesis 40:14–15.) But it soon became obvious that Joseph's hope had failed; there would be no pardon. Instead, Joseph's release from prison was delayed two more long and painful years. From a natural perspective, the reason for this delay was simple enough: The butler, Joseph's hastily appointed lawyer, "did not...remember Joseph, but forgot him" (v. 23). From a spiritual viewpoint, however, the reason was quite different. What looked to be the cruel blow of an indifferent man was in fact the calculated act of a loving God. Consider these thoughts.

Joseph's primary work was to save the chosen people and all nations by making preparations for the approaching worldwide famine. If he had been released before the time of Pharaoh's dreams (Gen. 41:1), he would probably have left Egypt and returned to his father in Palestine. Then, when the great famine struck, he would have been far from his predestined place of service (Egypt) and totally inaccessible to the key man God had called him to assist (Pharaoh). The two-year delay, therefore, served God's purpose by holding Joseph in place until his season of fruitfulness arrived. During that period, Joseph was God's deliverer-in-waiting. Pharaoh could easily call for him at a moment's notice and, upon realizing his exceptional wisdom and divine gifts of interpretation and organization, appoint him prime minister of Egypt. And when

Joseph's moment of greatest personal advantage finally arrived, that's exactly what Pharaoh did. (See Genesis 41:14–44.)

After Joseph's dramatic royal appointment, God's wise plan was laid bare for all to see. In His all-powerful goodness, God had arranged circumstances so that the most powerful man in the world, Pharaoh, and indeed the whole world itself, had a desperate need for the very gifts that only Joseph possessed. Hence, when the time came to begin preparing for the famine, God set a chain of events in motion: He gave Pharaoh his epic dreams; Pharaoh's counselors failed to interpret them; Pharaoh's butler remembered Joseph's gifts and recommended him to Pharaoh; Pharaoh called for Joseph; Joseph interpreted Pharaoh's dreams and proposed an inspired famine preparation plan; and Pharaoh and his counselors agreed that Joseph was the best man to implement the plan.

Thus in God's time, which was the hour of Joseph's greatest personal advantage, Joseph's gifts made room for him and brought him before great men. (See Proverbs 18:16.) And suddenly he became the world's man of the hour—and one of its most powerful and privileged inhabitants. A promotion more amazing than Joseph's cannot be imagined. He went from prison to palace overnight!

~

In these three examples, God purposely deferred His help until the moment that was most advantageous for His servants. With great care He coordinated all things together to do the utmost in behalf of His long-tried children. How unselfish He was! He did these things, not for His glory or pleasure but solely to enlarge His servants' sense of fulfillment and personal joy: "that your joy may be full" (John 16:24). With singular purpose He sought only their good: "to do thee good at thy latter end" (Deut. 8:16). His aim was purely to increase their blessings, to make their rewards finer, more numerous and more satisfying. Truly, as Isaiah declared, He delayed His inter-vention only that He might be more gracious unto them: "And therefore will the LORD wait, that he may be gracious unto you …that he may have mercy upon you" (Isa. 30:18).

And the good news is the Lord stands ready to do the same today for all who wait for Him: "Blessed are *all* they that wait for him" (Isa. 30:18, emphasis added).

WILL YOU BELIEVE FOR AND AWAIT YOUR DIVINE INTERVENTION DIVINELY TIMED?

Have you grown "weary in well doing" (Gal. 6:9) of late? Has the trial of your faith reached and then surpassed the limit of your personal patience? Having done all, are you standing firm spiritually, being still and knowing that the Lord is God—and yet He still has not come to your aid? Has con-templation of this caused you, as Peter did, to slip and begin to sink beneath your troubled waters? Then follow these simple instructions.

First, remember that the Lord's tarrying is never acci-dental. He could send legions of angels this instant to get you out of your troubles, but if He did so, how could He achieve His purposes in your trial? That is, how could He develop your faith to its maximum potential? How could He give you His very best blessings?

Second, refocus your mind's eye on what He so earnestly seeks to do in you and for you. Passionately, He seeks to deliver you forever from all your nagging fears and establish in you faith of the highest order. The apostle Peter described this divine desire: "But the God of all grace…after ye have suffered awhile, make you perfect, |establish|, strengthen, settle you" (1 Pet. 5:10; see James 1:4). And, patiently, He is working for you, steadily coordinating all things—your circumstances and many others'—for your lasting good. He is denying you good things presently only to give you the best things permanently.

Third, believe these truths passionately, and patiently await the Lord's intervention in your life. It's one thing to know a truth and another thing to deeply believe it. True belief is always accompanied by committal—we act upon or rest in the truth we know, then rely on God to respond in His time and way.

Fourth, watch that you don't fall into the subtle twin-snares of offense and self-pity. Many believers before you have had to wait long for the Lord's help, many others are doing so right now, and still others will do so after you're gone. So don't pet your poor, pitiful, persecuted self as if your trial were unique! (See 1 Corinthians 10:13.) Instead, thank the Lord for giving you an *opportunity* to keep the word of His patience. (See Revelation 3:10.)

~

If you do these things, you will surely experience divine intervention divinely timed, for the divine Intervener never fails. When that moment arrives, all the puzzling pieces of your dilemma will suddenly fall into place to form a beautiful scene, filled with comforting favor and joyous fulfillments. God's perfectly orchestrated symphony of events will reach a glorious crescendo, at which time He will shower you with far more blessings than you ever imagined possible. As the apostle Paul wrote, God will do "exceedingly abundantly above all that we ask or think, according to the power that worketh in us" (Eph. 3:20).

Truly, if you wait for divine deliverance divinely timed, you will find it well worth your wait. Then, after you get your victory, don't lose it.

Chapter Nineteen

THE AFTER-BATTLE

Wherefore, let him that thinketh he standeth take heed lest he fall.

—1 CORINTHIANS 10:12

Surprisingly, our most vulnerable moments often arise not during but after our most demanding tests. On Galilee's raging waters we walk calmly in faith with little difficulty and not even the slightest fear of falling. But after we arrive at the other side of our stormy trial, little things trip us up. Why is this?

When imposing spiritual storms appear on the horizons of our lives, sensing danger, we realize we must quickly get into our best spiritual condition. Consequently, we shift into our spiritual "hurricane preparation" mode—our highest level of sanctification. Energetically, we recall and put to use every spiritual lesson we've ever learned. We watch, we pray and we eschew evil. We confess our sins, forgive our offenders and make restitution to any we have wronged. We pay old vows, make new ones and diligently discharge our duties, rising early and working late, if necessary, to do so. We forsake worldliness, fast from distractions and feed on the things that edify. We humbly worship and read our Bibles with meditation. We fervently plead God's promises, carefully obeying their conditions and confessing our faith aloud. Thus with urgency we gird up the loins of our souls. Driven by the knowledge that Satan's buffetings will soon test us to the limit, we determine to be our best the moment his challenge arrives. As a result, when the storm breaks, we don't. Inspired and focused, we trust and obey our Deliverer all the way through our turbulent episode until it finally ends. Then, once more, all is calm.

In that moment of relief the thought comes, ever so subtly: The worst is over, so why keep our spiritual habits going? Why not let up? This idea is certainly welcome, and it's reasonable. After all, we've been under a sustained, severe strain and deserve a break. Besides, we've won! The enemy tested our stand, and we stood his test: We're still standing! He rocked our boat, but it still arrived safely at the other side. And best of all, we've now walked on stormy water, as Peter did. What a victory God has given and we have taken! As enjoyable as it is, this soaring consciousness of victory often renders us unconsciously vulnerable. It is the very attitude the apostle Paul had in mind when he penned his warning:

> Wherefore, let him that thinketh he standeth take heed lest he fall.
>
> —1 Corinthians 10:12

Yielding, we relax our spiritual vigilance and fall back into that "lukewarm Laodicean" mode so widely scorned—and too often enjoyed—among us. Degeneration begins when we start leaving off private time with the Lord, neglecting our vital fellowship with Him in His Word and in prayer. As it worsens we forget our vows, desert our duties and give ourselves over to distractions. Most dangerously, however, we stop screening our thoughts. Unchecked, our imaginations rove, and our emotions swing back and forth. Soon we've lost everything we gained during our impassioned pre-trial preparations. Our minds are left dull, and our spirits, weak. Sensing our weakened state (see chapter 4), the enemy then places a snare before us, and down we go, as Peter did, into a dangerous spiritual sinking spell of failure, discouragement and more failure.

What a surprising fall! Only a few days—even hours—earlier we basked in glowing thoughts of how well we had stood our test; now we're under the waves and beginning to drown. What has happened? It's very simple. We won the big battle, but the after-battle, subtle as it was, took us. We stood strong in the main test and we knew it, but because we stopped taking heed to ourselves, we fell. The danger undertows pose to swimmers at the beach further illustrates this.

THE UNDERTOW

In the surf, the swimmer is faced with two basic problems: the waves and the undertow.

The waves, highly visible and strong, are his big test. If not detected, they can easily knock him off his feet. To avoid this he must either dive under or leap over the breakers as they come—or brace himself for a watery collision. Lest these obvious buffetings overcome him, he summons all his powers to withstand.

After each wave passes, calm settles in for the moment. The danger seems to have passed with the punch and roar of the surging whitecaps. But it hasn't. A second enemy, and with it a second battle, lurks beneath the surface.

That foe is the undertow—an underwater current

moving in a direction different from the surface waters, usually heading out to sea. Though not a visible enemy like the waves, the undertow is just as threatening. If not respected, it can be deadly. A strong undertow can easily pull under small children and drown them. A riptide can even drag experienced adult swimmers far from shore and safety if they are tired, weak or not vigilant. Hence, even when he thinks he stands, the wise swimmer takes heed, ever ready for the after-battle of the surf.

Wise Christians do the same, for they know if they fail to watch, even the strongest believers can be moved by the power of spiritual undertow. Let's consider some biblical victims of spiritual undertow.

VICTIMS OF SPIRITUAL UNDERTOW

Elijah

Elijah's greatest spiritual victory occurred on Mount Carmel. (See 1 Kings 18.) It was there God granted the fiery intervention that ended the prophet's long standoff with the advocates of Baal worship and cleared the way for righteousness to revisit the land of Israel. Yet, incredibly, it was just after his greatest victory that Elijah took his greatest fall.

Only hours after Elijah returned to Jezreel, the enemy struck back with an unexpected undercurrent of trouble. By way of Jezebel's death threat, Satan grabbed the heels of God's inspired spokesman and pulled—"So let the gods do to me, and more also, if I make not thy life as the life of one of them [the slain prophets of Baal] by tomorrow about this time" (1 Kings 19:2). Surprisingly, Jezebel's words prevailed against the formerly immovable prophet. Uncharacteristically, Elijah failed to respond in faith to Jezebel's words. The result? A man of extraordinary faith fell prey to the ordinary fear of man. The courageous preacher who had withstood nationwide rejection for three years turned and, as a common coward, "went for his life" (v. 3), forfeiting both his wide ministry and God's glorious visitation already in progress. Thus we are left pondering this amazing Bible fact: Elijah's most ruinous defeat occurred only hours after his most rousing victory.

Noah

Noah stood firm against two spiritual tidal waves—first, by preparing the world's only ark while surrounded by disbelieving neighbors; second, by enduring an entire year of confinement in the ark during the terrifying flood. (See Genesis 6–8.) Thus, along with his family, he faced and successfully passed the two most imposing swells of stress the world had ever known. Yet after Noah's twin walls of water passed, a subtler yet more effective current stirred beneath their wake.

After his release from the ark, Noah made wine from his vintage. (See Genesis 9:20.) While enjoying his newly fermented beverage, he overindulged to the point of drunkenness and carelessly exposed himself before his sons (vv. 21–24). So we discover another surprising revelation: The spiritual undertow pulled Noah down into his most shameful failure not long after he reveled in his most glorious achievement of faith.

Abraham

Abraham was suddenly confronted by an imposing swell of judgment when the Lord unexpectedly visited him and announced He was about to destroy Sodom and Gomorrah. (See Genesis 18.) But, ever the believer, Abraham braced himself for its impact by offering immediate and persistent prayer for his wayward nephew, Lot, whose unguarded life was in great danger in Sodom. Thanks to his persistent prayers, God delivered Lot in the day He overwhelmed Sodom. (See Genesis 19.)

Yet soon after God's destructive wave of judgment

passed, Abraham made an uncharacteristic and self-opposing move. Impulsively, and without divine authorization, he relocated his family in Gerar and, once there, lied to Abimelech about Sarah. (See Genesis 20.) So we see more of the above: Shortly after his greatest prayer triumph, Abraham fell headlong into the snares of self-led living and falsehood.

~

Each of these saints succeeded in high-pressure tests, only to fail afterwards in low-pressure scenarios. They won their battles, but lost their after-battles. To avoid repeating their falls, we must understand the nature of our after-battles.

THE ESSENCE OF OUR AFTER-BATTLES

In their essence, after-battles are subtle post-trial thought conflicts. They begin with the assumption that because the intense stress of our trial has passed, we can let down our guards without fear of further attack. So we forsake the vital duties of spiritual vigilance and self-examination, but this leaves the doors to our souls wide open, unguarded and very vulnerable. Any of a host of lying thoughts may then easily walk in and begin to move and lead us. These satanic intruders are false notions such as:

- A little disobedience won't make any difference (see chapter 16, page 166);
- We don't have to be diligent *every* day;
- God is just too gracious and kind-hearted to withhold from us or to punish us for sin.

They may also be wrong attitudes and emotions such as:

- Anger, fear, anxiety, unmercifulness or envy.

Whatever the subversive undertow, always our minds are the point of attack in our after-battles. Always, the enemy tries to grip our thought center and pull us down with misleading ideas or corruptive attitudes. Because these quiet assaults don't arrive with the noisy fanfare of big tests, or roar and foam and hit hard like powerful waves, we may not pay them any attention. But that's not wise because, as shown above, after-battles are just as dangerous as major battles. Why? Because one wrong thought yielded to can turn a life and ruin a destiny. David is a case in point.

DAVID'S AFTER-BATTLE

David learned the danger of after-battles the hard way. After being bitterly persecuted by King Saul for many years, David one day found his chief enemy encamped, sleeping and vulnerable (1 Sam. 26). Immediately, he faced a difficult choice: Should he avenge himself or trust God to deal with Saul in His own time and way? It was a great test—and very public. Both David's and Saul's men were present, witnessing every word and act. Wisely, David chose not to harm his enemy but to appeal to him instead, hoping his open display of love would lead Saul to repent (vv. 9–20). Saul did acknowledge his guilt and David's goodness, but he stopped short of repentance (vv. 21–25). Afterward, Saul and David each returned to their respective domains—Saul to his court at Gibeah and David to his fugitive lifestyle in the wilderness of Judea. So another big battle came and went. Thank God, the pressure was now off.

But as time passed, to David's disappointment, Saul remained unchanged. Then, quietly, a seemingly harmless little thought drifted into David's mind: "And David said in his heart, I shall now perish one day by the hand of Saul" (1 Sam. 27:1). Uncharacteristically, David failed to bring this satanic lie—a direct contradiction of God's clear promise that David would be Israel's next king (1 Sam. 16:1–13)—into subjection to the divine truth he had held dear for many years. Consequently, just when David thought he had stood his test, he fell. First, he fell into doubt and unbelief in God: "I shall now perish one day by the hand of Saul [that is, God's promise will never come to pass]" (1 Sam. 27:1). Second, he fell into carnal reasoning and selfish planning: "There is nothing better for me than that I should speedily escape into the land of the Philistines, and Saul shall despair of me, to seek me any more. ..so shall I escape out of his hand" (v. 1). Third, he fell into foolish, self-opposing action: "And David arose, and he passed over...unto Achish, the son of Maoch, king of Gath" (v. 2). Israel's anointed king wasted sixteen precious months in Philistia (v. 7). Only by God's severe-yet-merciful chastisement was he saved from his after-battle (See 1 Samuel 30:1–20.)

Like David, we sometimes fall into depression after victorious confrontations with our detractors. The reason? We lose the after-battle! In the wake of our big crises, we began rethinking things—our adversaries' mean-spirited intentions, the unfairness and hypocrisy of their actions, their stinging words and haughty attitudes, their stubborn refusal to change, God's apparent indifference and slowness to help us, the fact that He still has not fulfilled His promises and so on. Consequently, even though our big battle has ended, these thoughts revive its essential spiritual struggle. We withstood heavy spiritual waves the first time they struck; now they've returned, like surprisingly strong subsurface currents, to try us again. And if we don't deal with them by closely obeying God's Word, they will deal with us. Like David, down we will go.

How to Fight and Win Your After-Battles

A veteran of many after-battles, the apostle Paul left us clear instructions on how to fight and win our after-battles. According to his writings, obedience in our thought lives—maintained by thorough self-examination, or the screening of every thought and emotion that enters our consciousness—is the key to victory. (See 2 Corinthians 10:3–5.) Anticipating the subtle flow of unspiritual thoughts that challenge us in the aftermath of our trials, Paul wrote:

> Casting down imaginations, and every high thing that exalteth itself against the knowledge of God, and bringing into captivity every thought to the obedience of Christ.
>
> —2 CORINTHIANS 10:5

Analysis of this verse reveals that it contains two closely related commands:

1. Cast down "imaginations" and "high things."

"Imaginations" include a whole host of unhealthy mental images, also thoughts that are unreal—not clearly identifiable as facts. Imaginations include:

- Anxious thoughts about the future, including and arising from predictions, daydreams or any other kind of worrisome thoughts (See Matthew 6:25–34; Philippians 4:6–7.)

- Captivating mental "video replays" of unpleasant scenes, words and actions, which typically stir anger and vengeance

- Self-depreciating mental "reruns" of our failures, which breed discouragement, unbelief and further failures

- Self-congratulatory mental "reruns" of our victories, which inflate us with pride or arrogance

- Suppositions of what others may be thinking or saying about us, or of their hidden motives, including hearsay

When received, these imaginations produce spiritual destabilization. They stir sinful emotions, sully holiness and weaken faith, leaving us shaken, confused and unsound. We

203

cannot be believers of "sound mind" (2 Tim. 1:7) if we let them have the run of our mind. The same is true for "high things."

High things are thoughts and concepts that rise up against divine authority in our lives and seek to hinder or destroy our fellowship with God. Specifically, they lift themselves above God's Word or attempt to undermine our trust in and love of God Himself. Among these are:

- Thoughts of pride, vanity or unkindness
- Doubt or outright unbelief in God's Word
- Reasonings that question God's actions, judgments or motives
- Rebellious thoughts—that incline us to despise meekness, humility or submission to authority and hence prompt us to disrespect and resist our human authorities or defy God's authority by disobeying His revealed will

When received, such high thoughts produce in us a high mind—a satanic attitude that is unruly to God and inconsiderate of others. In this proud state, our fellowship with Jesus Christ is broken, and our usefulness to Him is quenched.

For this reason, Paul instructed us to rid ourselves of imaginations and high things quickly—very quickly. To "cast down" something is to immediately fling it away, not slowly observe and handle it. Hence, it is the opposite of meditation—holding thoughts in our minds and consciously pondering them. Why is this important? Because, from a spiritual perspective, what we think, we are. To let sin rest in our thoughts is to let sin and Satan abide in our lives. (See Proverbs 23:7.) Are we casting down or considering the imaginations and high things that seek to enter our minds?

2. Take every thought captive to obey the Word of God.

Here we are told to let the Scriptures be the MPs

(military police) that stand guard over the entrances of our spiritual bases of operation—our souls. Every time a thought or emotion seeks entrance into our souls, we momentarily halt it and judge it by the standard of the Holy Word, which reveals perfectly what God accepts. (See Psalm 139:23–24.) If the thought or emotion doesn't line up with that standard, we arrest it; that is, we mentally handcuff it and cast it out of our minds by a brief moment of quiet-but-strong rejection. Internally, we give a clear and final order to our hostile intruder: "I reject you. You will not rest in my soul." Meanwhile, everything that meets the standard of righteousness expressed in Scripture is allowed to enter our internal spiritual bases. (See Philippians 4:8.)

So we conclude: When we are challenged by subtle unspiritual thoughts and emotions, the speed and persistence with which we halt them and subsequently begin to think, confess and obey New Testament counter-thoughts determines whether we stand or fall in the after-battle. The quick stand; the slow fall. The persistent prevail; the inconsistent fail.

⌒

Awareness of our after-battles need not leave us anxious and worried. We can and should rest after our victories—but in a humble attitude of thankfulness and vigilance, not one of foolish pride and mental sloth. While an occasional change of pace is helpful from a physical standpoint, a spiritual letup—a foolish excursion into the forbidden territory of sinful thinking or living—is debilitating and dangerous. Wise Christians understand that the price of constant strength is constant vigilance. Like Gideon's soldiers, therefore, we must always be watchful, ever mindful of our thoughts, feelings and reactions to daily life. Christ's parting words confirm this.

Among the last words Jesus spoke to His apostles were a series of exhortations to watchfulness:

And take heed to yourselves...*Watch* ye, therefore, and pray always.

—LUKE 21:34–36, EMPHASIS ADDED

Watch, therefore....

—MATTHEW 25:13, EMPHASIS ADDED

Take heed, *watch* and pray...*Watch* ye, therefore...And what I say unto you I say unto all, *Watch*.

—MARK 13:33–37, EMPHASIS ADDED

Typically, parting words are those a speaker considers most important. That Jesus commanded us to watch for His appearing implies we must also watch over our souls; only those who vigilantly guard their hearts truly watch for Christ. With Jesus' last words before us, let us determine to always watch over our souls—before the battle, during the battle and after the battle. As diligent self-examiners, we will never be caught off guard by the prince of the after-battle. When he tries to quietly trip us up, we will quietly check him. And instead of sinking, we will continue walking with Jesus on the troubled waters of life...until we reach the end of our personal testing process.

Chapter Twenty

THERE IS AN END TO TESTING

Now I know…

—GENESIS 22:12

Genesis 22 opens with the memorable words, "God did |test| Abraham" (Gen. 22:1). And test Abraham He did.

But as we will see in this final chapter, not all divine tests are created equal. There are differing degrees of difficulty: elementary, secondary and advanced. The test Abraham faced in Genesis 22 was unquestionably advanced. In fact, it was his grand finale, his most difficult—and last—spiritual examination. With it, God brought to a close the lengthy proving process He began the day He called Abraham out of Ur of the Chaldees. When God saw Abraham's trust and obedience acted out to the last word, step and reach on Mount Moriah,

He voiced His full and final approval of the patriarch's trial-forged character: "*Now I know* that thou fearest God" (v. 12, emphasis added). These words were Abraham's commencement, his graduation *summa cum laude*, from God's School of the Spirit. Hence, thereafter his demanding trials ceased. Never again did Abraham experience a serious spiritual crisis. The remainder of his days were spent gloriously free from the agitating adversities that for so many years had visited him regularly. Now why should this interest us?

It concerns us because Abraham is the spiritual forefather of every Christian: "Know ye, therefore, that they who are of faith, the same are the |sons| of Abraham" (Gal. 3:7). Consequently, his testing process foreshadows ours. Let's review his major trials (Genesis 12–22) so we may know what kinds of trials the Heavenly Examiner will send us and, more importantly, so we may be confident that one day, as Abraham's did, our trials will end.

TEST #1: SEPARATION FROM COUNTRY AND KINDRED

"Now the Lord had said unto Abram, Get thee out of thy country, and from thy kindred, and from thy father's house, unto a land that I will show thee" (Gen. 12:1). By forcing him to choose between good things and best things, God's first command to Abraham (here Abram) created his first test. To have the best relationship—a personal walk with God—Abraham would have to "get thee out" from the good relationships he had known all his life; that meant separation from his moon-worshiping countrymen and his own beloved but unbelieving family members. To have the best country—the land God promised to give him—he would have to depart from the good country he had lived in since birth. Wisely, Abraham made the right choice. He looked beyond the good and began focusing on the best. By faith,

208

he committed himself to his new Friend and departed to seek his new country—and life. Thus, abandoning all his old associations, he embraced his new and fascinating association with God: "So Abram departed" (v. 4). Thus began a great quest: The earthling Abraham was heaven bound.

Similarly, the Holy Spirit calls every newly born-again one to "come out" of his former Babylon, or personal world of sin:

> Be ye not unequally yoked together with unbelievers... Wherefore, *come out from among them*, and be ye separate, saith the Lord...and I will receive you, and will be a Father unto you.
> —2 CORINTHIANS 6:14–18, EMPHASIS ADDED

For some this will mean a personal exodus, a physical departure from former companions in sin. (See 1 Peter 4:3–4.) For others it will mean domestic spiritual war, a painful break from relatives who are openly hostile and actively subversive toward their new faith. This is the "sword" Christ plainly prophesied would visit some families. (See Matthew 10:34–39.) For still others it will mean not a physical separation but an uncomfortable internal division created by the arrival of a new life, a new Lord and a new biblical viewpoint. For all, it will mean abandoning expectations of being understood and respected by family or friends who reject Jesus' lordship and dishonor His Word.

Obeying God's call will also mean adopting a new viewpoint toward our homeland: "Get thee out of thy *country*" (emphasis added). Spiritual rebirth enlarges the scope of our affections from one to all nations. Because the Holy Spirit's love is worldwide ("For God so loved the *world*," John 3:16, emphasis added), we are no longer limited by our formerly narrow patriotic prejudices. Taking the viewpoint of our new Lord and Master, who is no respecter of persons or nations, we now love not only our native land but all nations for whom

Christ died. So, enlarged from nationalists to international-ists, we launch out on our great spiritual journey.

TEST #2: FAMINE INSTEAD OF FEAST

After having taken up his cross to follow God, Abraham no doubt expected some kind of favorable response. And why shouldn't he? The Lord had explicitly promised to bless him greatly and make him a great man (Gen. 12:2–3), and he had obeyed, so blessing, prosperity and greatness were rightfully his! A herdsman, Abraham surely anticipated growing flocks and great feasts in Canaan. But instead of blessing, Abraham found a paradox—adversity in the land of prosperity. Famine, not feasting, was his portion from God: "And there was a famine in the land" (v. 10). Baffled by this contradic-tion, Abraham promptly failed this, his second test of faith. Rather than pray, believe and wait for God's help, he sought support from the nearest and most logical world-source—the wisdom and wealth of Egypt. Thus our father in faith failed to live by faith. Obviously his belief in God, though real, was weak. He simply wasn't ready yet to trust God for his daily bread.

We too may be taken aback by our initial Christian expe-riences. After surrendering our lives to Jesus, we naturally and scripturally expect His blessing. Yet the same Bible that reveals God's desire to bless us discloses His age-old intention to test our faith. When our fruitful fields turn out to be stony ground, when our initial high hopes produce nothing, our joy in the Word withers into bland disillusionment. We think to ourselves, *This Christianity thing isn't panning out the way I thought it would*. Then it's time to decide if and why we want to go further in the Way.

Do we want to serve God's purpose or ours? Do we want to walk by faith or trust solely in the ways and means of man? Do we demand comfort always, or are we willing to endure the disruption of God's testing process—and to one day bring Him glory?

TEST #3: SEPARATION FROM CARNAL BRETHREN

After leaving the idolatrous inhabitants of Ur, Abraham's separation seemed complete. But it wasn't. Another holy severance lay ahead.

Abraham's nephew, Lot, had followed Abraham when he answered the call of God: "So Abram departed, as the Lord had spoken unto him; *and Lot went with him*" (Gen. 12:4, emphasis added). Though, like Abraham, Lot was saved (see 2 Peter 2:7–8), he was still more fascinated with the things of this world than the things of God. Hence self-interest, not the Lord, was his true god. Eventually, the day came when Lot's god called and he answered, leaving the company of the faithful to seek commercial gain and social prominence in unfaithful Sodom. (See Genesis 13:10–11.) Knowing that Sodom was rife with homosexuality, Abraham made no attempt to accompany or visit Lot there. So the two formerly united brethren went their separate ways: "And Lot journeyed east: and they *separated* themselves the one from the other" (v. 11, emphasis added; see verse 14). By continuing to walk with God when Lot walked away from God, Abraham passed his next test. He stayed true to the Lord when others turned aside.

Inevitably, fully surrendered disciples of Christ experience similar partings of the ways. How wonderful it would be if all our brethren followed the Lord all the way through life, but the fact remains that many turn back: "From that time many of his disciples went back, and walked no more with him" (John 6:66). Essentially, Christian discipleship is a matter of individual choice. When your Christian friends turn back to serve the sins and gods of this Sodom-like world (see 2 Timothy 4:10), what will you do? Will you follow

Abraham's footsteps and those of the devoted hymnist, who vowed:

> I have decided to follow Jesus…
> The world behind me, the cross before me…
> Though none go with me, still I will follow…[1]

Jesus Himself wants to know: "Will ye also go away?" (John 6:67).

Test #4: Mercy for the Undeserving

The Scripture suggests that Lot also knew of Sodom's wickedness when he decided to live there. After stating that "Lot…pitched his tent toward Sodom" (Gen. 13:12), the very next statement reads, "But the men of Sodom were wicked and sinners before the Lord exceedingly" (v. 13). So we may assume that Lot's move was made in full light of Sodom's notorious reputation as a center of homosexuality. (Even today certain cities are notorious for specific kinds of vice. It is unthinkable that a Christian would choose to live in one without knowing of its iniquity.) By choosing to live in Sodom, Lot departed from the Lord's protection. Among sinners he exposed himself to dangers he would never have experienced among saints.

One such danger erupted when foreign armies captured Sodom and fled with its spoils, including Lot, his family and their possessions. (See Genesis 14:1–12.) This posed yet another test for Abraham. In his righteous mind, the issue was very clear: For choosing to live among sinners, Lot deserved punishment. Both Sodom's fall and Lot's captivity were divine judgments. Why, then, should Abraham and his men have to risk their lives to deliver Lot from well-deserved judgment? They shouldn't. And they didn't; God did not order Abraham to intervene. Yet, surprisingly, Abraham chose to do what he didn't have to do—show mercy to the undeserving. In a remarkable demonstration of divine grace through human agency, Abraham and his 318 militarily untrained servants pursued Lot's captors (a formidable and experienced military force) and defeated them, freeing Lot and his family and restoring their property (vv. 13–16). Thus a worthy servant of God helped an unworthy one in his hour of need.

Are we prepared to do the same? Will we kindly assist the undeserving ones God sends our way? They will test our kindness, patience and faith to the limit, but if we will not fail to show them the love of God, the God of love will not fail to show kindness to two especially unworthy ones: you and me.

TEST #5: WAITING LONG FOR GOD'S FULFILLMENT

In Genesis 15–16 we find Abraham enduring a lengthy trial of patience. Long after God explicitly promised to bless his "seed" (Gen. 12:7), Abraham still had no son through whom God's promise could be performed. Wearied by years of waiting, and still childless, he poured out his complaint before the Lord: "Lord GOD, what wilt thou give me, seeing I go childless, and the |heir| of my house is this Eliezer of Damascus?" (Gen. 15:2). God responded by graciously clarifying His promise. Eliezer was not the son of promise: "This [Eliezer] shall not be thine heir" (v. 4). Another heir would be given, a true son, fathered by Abraham: "But he that shall come forth out of thine own |loins| shall be thine heir." So, with his vision now clearer and brighter, Abraham continued waiting patiently for God's fulfillment.

But after ten years, Abraham's patience began wearing thin. Then Sarah had a good idea: Abraham should take a concubine. That was how other Canaanite couples conquered barrenness; why should they not do the same? Ever so subtly, Abraham was again put to a test. Should he continue trusting God to fulfill His promise in His own time and way, or should he yield to the popular wisdom and ways of his culture? Undoubtedly something in him whispered, "Wait," but another voice cried, "Act," arguing that a concubine would be a more reasonable—and quicker—solution to his distressing seed problem. Sarah's offer of her handmaid Hagar seemed a very convenient, possibly even a divine confirmation to this second voice. So Abraham yielded to Sarah's counsel...and so he failed his test of patience. As good as Sarah's idea was, it wasn't good enough because it wasn't God's. Because He had not authorized Abraham's union with Hagar, God refused to honor it. Ishmael was soon born but never blessed. Also, God chastened Abraham for his refusal to await His time; for thirteen years He did not speak to him. (See Genesis 16:16–17:1.)

As He did with Abraham, the Lord gives every Christian a chance to keep the word of His patience. Are we trusting and waiting for God to work, or are we reasoning and working in our own wisdom and strength? Is the Lord rewarding our patience by speaking to us regularly through His Word, or is He chastening us with painful silence?

TEST #6: A TEST OF CIRCUMCISION

When God ordered Abraham to submit himself, his male servants and his posterity to the rite of circumcision in Genesis 17:9–14, Abraham immediately obeyed (vv. 23–27). He knew that circumcision was not customary among the Canaanites and that compliance would cause his posterity to be considered different—and hence persecuted—by neighboring nations. But he willingly paid this price for righteousness' sake. He could live without man's approval if he had to, but not without God's. So, cutting away the flesh, he passed his test of loyalty.

Are we passing our tests? That is, are we living circumcised lives? In order to grow and please the Lord, are we cutting off pastimes, practices and interests that are purely worldly (see 1 John 2:15–17), and hence distractions and snares to our spiritual lives?

TEST #7: A TEST OF MERCY—AGAIN

After Abraham delivered him from captivity (see Genesis 14), Lot foolishly returned to his formerly low lifestyle in Sodom. Eventually the time came for God to judge sin's capital city and its lone redeemed-but-wayward citizen. Knowing Lot was dear to Abraham, apparently due to the latter's daily prayers, the Lord informed Abraham of a shocking secret: Sodom's full destruction was imminent. (See Genesis 18:16–21.) Abraham's thoughts then must have been interesting. Certainly, he knew Lot richly deserved judgment now more than ever. If he had been hardhearted, Abraham would have done nothing to change the divine sentence. But as seen in his earlier rescue of his backslidden nephew, Abraham was merciful. Hence, again he chose to help, this time by beseeching God to spare Sodom for Lot's sake. While not entirely successful, his persistent intercessions (vv. 22–33) nevertheless won Lot's release: "God remembered Abraham, and sent Lot out of the midst of the overthrow" (Gen. 19:29). Thus, by means of yet another test, Abraham's great mercy grew even greater.

His was a test we all eventually meet. Just when we think the Lots in our lives have finally learned to fear God and walk uprightly, they fall headlong into yet another dilemma and again need or call for help—*our* help. While we consider the numerous reasons we should *not* help our undeserving ones, the Holy Spirit quietly reminds us of His former mercies toward us. Then He reminds us of our former mercies toward them and whispers quietly, "Ditto." We get the point: God has done it for us before, and we have done it for Lot before, so we should just quietly do it again—with joy. "For God loveth a cheerful giver" (2 Cor. 9:7). So we pray and give and work until the Lord grants them yet another way of escape. No, it's not a waste; it's His way of making His love *in* us as big as His love *for* us.

Test #8: The Lapse at Gerar

As stated in chapter 19, saints are often vulnerable after great spiritual victories, and Abraham was no exception. After his Christlike intercession for Lot, Abraham reverted to surprisingly unspiritual behavior by wandering off into the land of Gerar without divine permission. (See Genesis 20.) It was a rare and unfruitful act of independence for a man so used to leaning on the everlasting arms. In Gerar, one sin quickly begot another. Moved by the fear of man, Abraham lied about Sarah to protect not her, but himself: "And Abraham said of Sarah, his wife, She is my sister" (v. 2). Suddenly, heaven's plan was in trouble. God had to personally intervene to keep the chosen mother of the son of promise pure: "But God came to Abimelech in a dream by night, and said to him, Behold, thou art but a dead man, for the woman whom thou hast taken; for she is a man's wife" (v. 3). Speaking for God, Abimelech ministered a stinging rebuke to Abraham (vv. 9–10), who then quietly returned to the place God put him in, his latest report card in hand clearly marked *F.*

At times we commit similar failures. After achieving a string of victories by faith, patience and love, we impulsively strike out on our own and manage to achieve fear, confusion and embarrassing failure. Immediately, by His Spirit, Christ's rebuke comes: "Apart from Me you can do nothing" (John 15:5, NAS). Then, thoroughly humiliated, we quietly resume walking with—not without—God.

Test #9: The Surrender of Ishmael and Hagar

Finally, Abraham's son of promise, Isaac, was born. (See Genesis 21:1–8.) But, as always, with blessing came conflict, this time in the form of jealousy.

When Hagar and Ishmael took exception to Sarah and her newborn son (v. 9), suddenly Abraham found himself in a painful dilemma. Should he try to hold things together and hope the unworkable would work out? Or should he, God forbid, physically separate his household's warring factions? God soon ended his quandary by sending a definitive word through Abraham's demanding wife, Sarah: "Cast out this bondwoman [Hagar] and her son" (v. 10). God then explained that because His blessing would come through Isaac, and not Ishmael, Hagar and Ishmael had to go: "And God said…in all that Sarah hath said unto thee, hearken unto her voice; for in Isaac shall thy seed by called" (v. 12). This grieved Abraham, who loved Ishmael dearly and had hoped that he would be blessed equally with Isaac (v. 11). But despite his sorrow, Abraham promptly yielded and paid the high price of obedience: "And Abraham rose up early in the morning, and took… Hagar…and gave her the child, and sent her away" (v. 14).

Sometimes, like Abraham, we grow very attached to our "Ishmaels"—or self-led works born solely of our wisdom, ways and strength. And because God permits them to remain for long periods in our lives, we assume they will remain permanently with His blessing. When reckoning day visits, will we pay whatever price heaven demands so our lives may be restored to divine order?

TEST #10: THE SURRENDER OF ISAAC (EVERYTHING!)

After sending away his firstborn, Abraham surely felt his greatest trial was behind him. Because his remaining son, Isaac, had been divinely tapped for blessing, Isaac was safe from the reach of divine testing. Or so it seemed.

But a surprising turn of events suddenly proved this assumption wrong. One shining morning God spoke these shocking words: "Take now thy son, thine only son Isaac, whom thou lovest, and get thee into the land of Moriah; and offer him there for a burnt offering upon one of the mountains which I will tell thee of" (Gen. 22:2). Suddenly, Abraham's world stood still. Everything he hoped for in life was invested

217

in Isaac, and now God said *kill him?* If God failed to bring Isaac through this baffling death-trial, all would be lost. Hence, with His call to sacrifice Isaac, God now required *everything* of Abraham, even his very dearest relationship and only remaining hope of blessing. This was the climax of Abraham's lifelong testing process, the summit of his lengthy grace-led, decision-by-decision, act-by-act climb to spiritual perfection. As of this moment, nothing—not a single possession, relationship or hope—had escaped the Divine Examiner's touch. God had asked everything of Abraham, and he had given it.

Jesus sounded this keynote when trumpeting His conditions for New Testament discipleship: "So likewise, whosoever he is of you that forsaketh not *all that he hath*, cannot be my disciple" (Luke 14:33, emphasis added). To most Christians in this Laodicean age, His note is a shrill and disturbing sound in our ears: To be a disciple, a believer must forsake "all that he hath"? What a shock! How can we, and why must we, give up everything? Abraham's lengthy course of trials, which was divinely planned, provides us with some clear answers.

First, Abraham didn't suddenly give up all that he had. As detailed in this chapter, his testing process touched every issue in his natural life (possessions, relationships, aspirations) gradually, one by one. Eventually, on Mount Moriah, everything had been dealt with. God will guide our testing process in the same way. He will test us thoroughly, issue by issue, and with increasing degrees of difficulty, until at last it can be said of us, as it was of Abraham, that we have put Jesus above "all that we have"—not sentimentally, but actually; not in will merely, but in practical life decisions; not by words only, but by irrevocable acts; not sporadically, but consistently.

Second, by requiring everything of Abraham, God proved the following:

- Abraham loved God more than anyone or anything.
- Abraham would trust God under any conditions.

- Abraham feared God and so would make any sacrifice rather than fail to do God's will.

Thus God knew beyond the shadow of a doubt that Abraham's character was perfect—spiritually mature, fully developed, finished. He was conformed to the image of the Son of God and so fit for His use.

The Lord gradually requires everything of us too for the same purposes—to prove He is indeed Lord of our lives, that we love Him supremely, trust Him completely and fear Him perfectly; to prove we are spiritually mature, lacking nothing; to prove we are fit for His use.

~

Notably, after Mount Moriah Abraham's fiery trials ceased, and they never returned. Moriah was Abraham's final proving ground! Similarly, every believer who follows on to know the Lord will have his or her final proving ground. Irrefutable Bible examples confirm this.

After his night in the den of lions, Daniel's severe trials ended; he never again faced anything so demanding. The same was true of Meshach, Shadrach and Abednego; after they emerged from Nebuchadnezzar's furnace, they were never again tried by fire. Joseph's lengthy series of trials terminated the day Pharaoh released him from prison, and it was never resumed. After the Christians of biblical Philadelphia finished keeping the word of His patience, Jesus promised them permanent exemption from tribulation: "Because thou hast kept the word of my patience, *I also will keep thee from the hour of temptation*, which shall come upon all the world, to try them that dwell upon the earth" (Rev. 3:10, emphasis added). These Word-facts refresh and refit us as we wearily trudge along toward our personal Moriah. Why?

Because they reassure us that, as Abraham's did, our testing process will end one day: "For surely there is an end"

(Prov. 23:18). When we arrive at the summit of our Christian maturity and have carried out our acts of trust and obedience to the last word, step and reach, God will say to us, "Now I know"—and all our demanding trials will cease.

~

In that day we will realize there is a purpose for all the pressure. Succinctly, it is *that we may be able to help other tried Christians*. God will then send us forth to strengthen others with the same truths that have strengthened us in our trials:

> The God of all comfort, who comforteth us in all our tribulation, that we may be able to comfort them who are in any trouble, by the comfort with which we ourselves are comforted of God.
>
> —2 CORINTHIANS 1:3–4

Peter's experience confirms this. After Peter walked successfully on the Sea of Galilee's stormy waters—surely New Testament symbolism for the highest kind of spiritual maturity, even equal to that which Abraham displayed on Mount Moriah—Christ led Peter and his fellow apostles straight to the far side of Galilee, where powerful and effective ministry ensued. (See Matthew 14:34–36; Mark 6:53–56.) Every Christian who learns to walk on water proficiently will experience a similar "afterwards." One day we will reach the far side of our Christian testing process. There, having retraced Peter's steps on water, we will retrace his steps on land—ministering strength and hope to our fellow believers by the power of the Spirit:

> And the Lord said…Satan hath desired to have you, that he may sift you as wheat; but I have prayed for thee, that thy faith fail not. And when thou art converted, *strengthen thy brethren*.
>
> —LUKE 22:31–32, EMPHASIS ADDED.

Thus our heavenly Father's plan will be complete. All the pressures of walking on water will at last have brought forth His full purpose in our lives.

Jesus set His face to go to Jerusalem because only there could He finish His Father's will on the cross. Follow His example today. Set your face to finish walking on your stormy waters, because only then will you become one who can strengthen your fellow believers.

Notes

Chapter Two
Seeing God in Everything

1. Mrs. C. Nuzum, *The Life of Faith* (Springfield, MO: Gospel Publishing House, 1928, 1956), 45.

Chapter Fourteen
Is Your Boat Full?

1. Taken in part from the sermon, "Don't Forget His Presence, Promise and Power," by R. W. Schambach.
2. "If" by Rudyard Kipling. Public domain. Taken from *The Best Loved Poems of the American People*, compiled by Hazel Felleman (Garden City, NY: Doubleday and Co., 1936), 65–66.
3. "Be Still, My Soul" by Katharina Von Schlegel. Public domain.
4. F. B. Meyer, *Elijah and the Secret of His Power* (Chicago: Moody Press, 1976), 5.

Chapter Sixteen
When the Righteous Repent

1. Oswald Chambers, *My Utmost for His Highest* (New York: Dodd, Mead and Company, Inc., 1935), 268.

Chapter Seventeen
Time to Do…Nothing

1. Will Steger, "Six Across Antarctica," *National Geographic* (November 1990): 66–93.

Chapter Twenty
There Is an End to Testing

1. "I Have Decided to Follow Jesus," author unknown. Public domain.

ABOUT THIS MINISTRY . . .

Mission Statement

Greg Hinnant Ministries is called to help train believers to walk in New Testament discipleship by teaching the timeless, priceless and unfailing principles of the Word of God. It is this ministry's earnest hope that in this way we may help prepare the body of Christ worldwide for, and so hasten, the appearing of our Lord Jesus Christ: "Prepare ye the way of the Lord" (Isa. 40:3).

Other Ministries Available

A monthly Bible message is available upon request to interested believers. Pastors and others in Christian ministry are particularly encouraged to take advantage of this mailing. Foreign readers are gladly served, with emphasis given to missionaries and others in the ministry.

The Lord has given Brother Greg many biblical messages, similar in length and style to the chapters in this book. These pieces are electronically stored and available for publication or distribution free of charge to interested Christian magazines, ministries and individuals.

If you are interested in having Greg Hinnant come share God's Word with your church, conference or Bible school, please do not hesitate to contact this ministry.

Contact Information

Greg Hinnant Ministries
P. O. Box 788
High Point, N.C. 27261

Tel.: (336) 882-1645
Fax: (336) 886-7227
E-mail: rghinnant@aol.com
(Area codes and e-mail address subject to change.)

Other Books by this Author

Walking in His Ways (Creation House Press)
Spiritual Truths for Overcoming Adversity